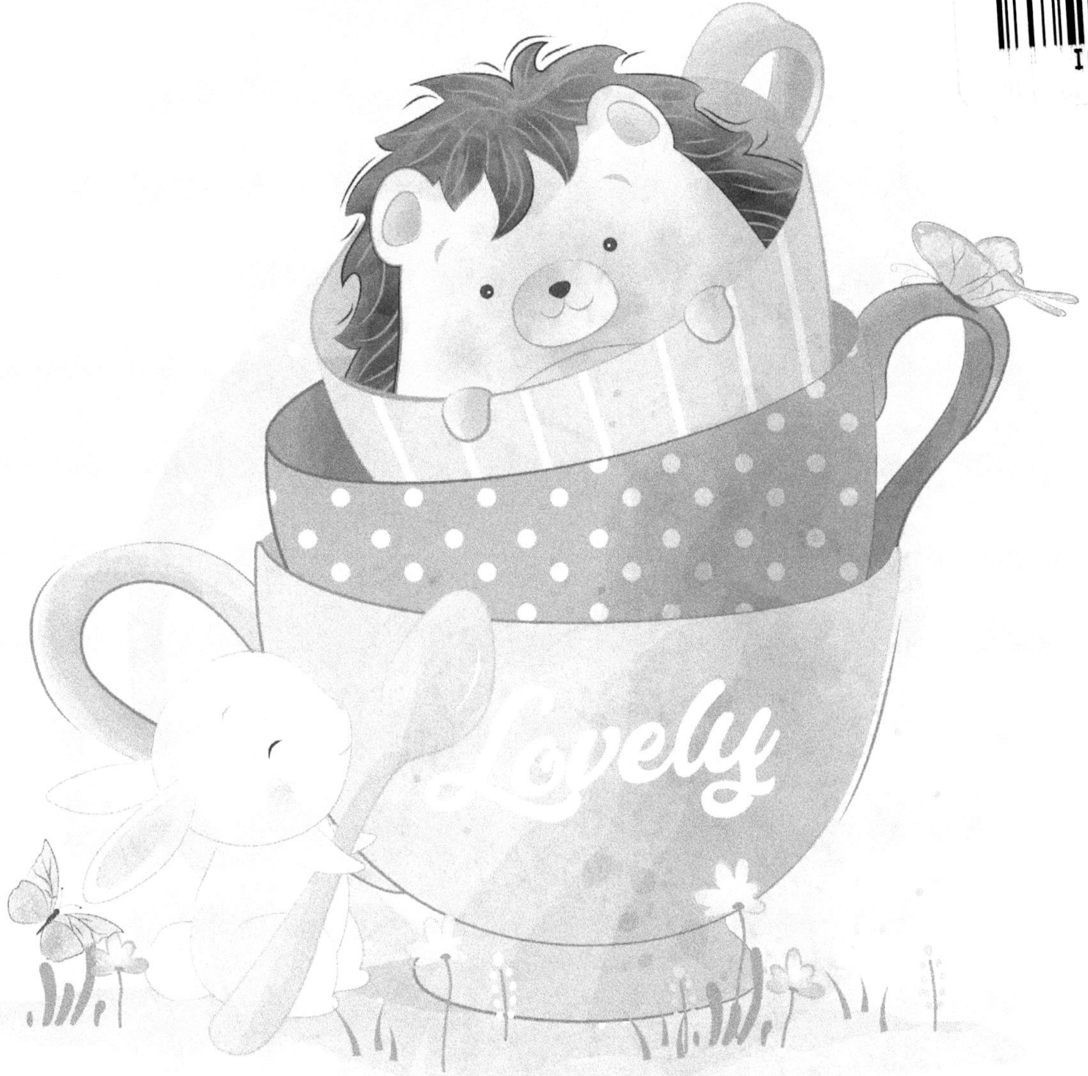


# HEDGEHOG

Lover Gifts

for Children, Girls & Boys

ARE

YOU

READY ?

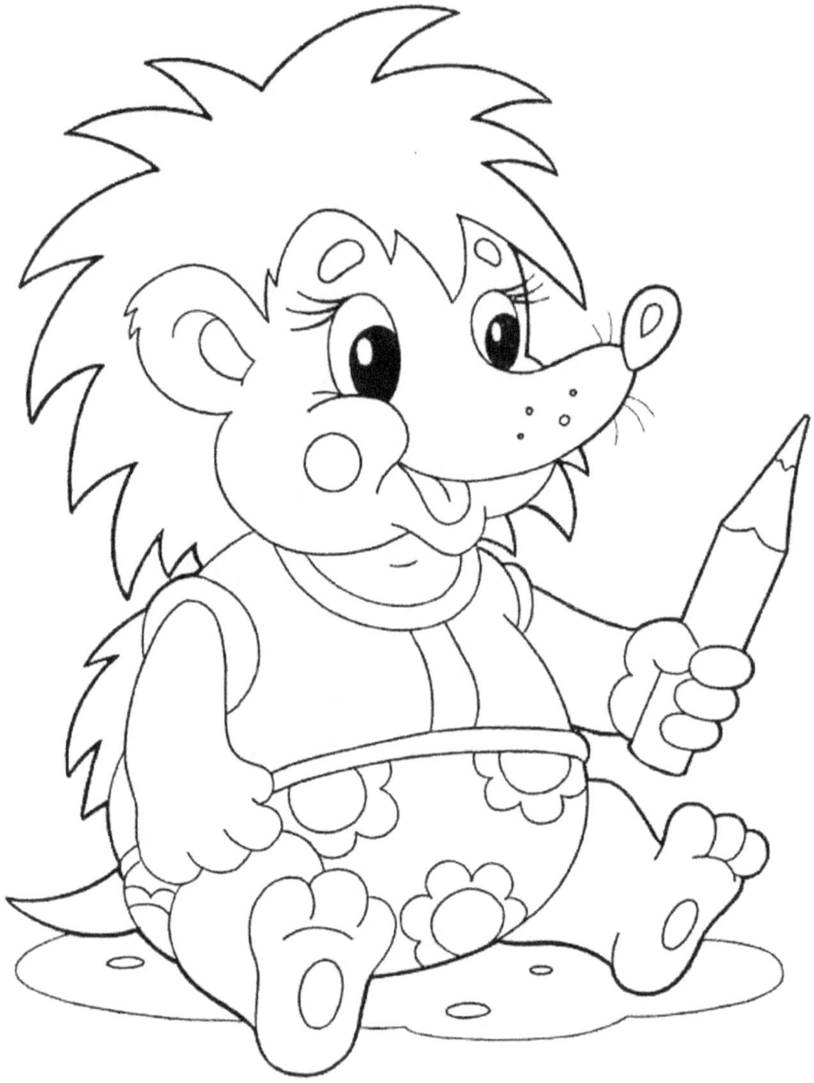

LET'S BEGIN!

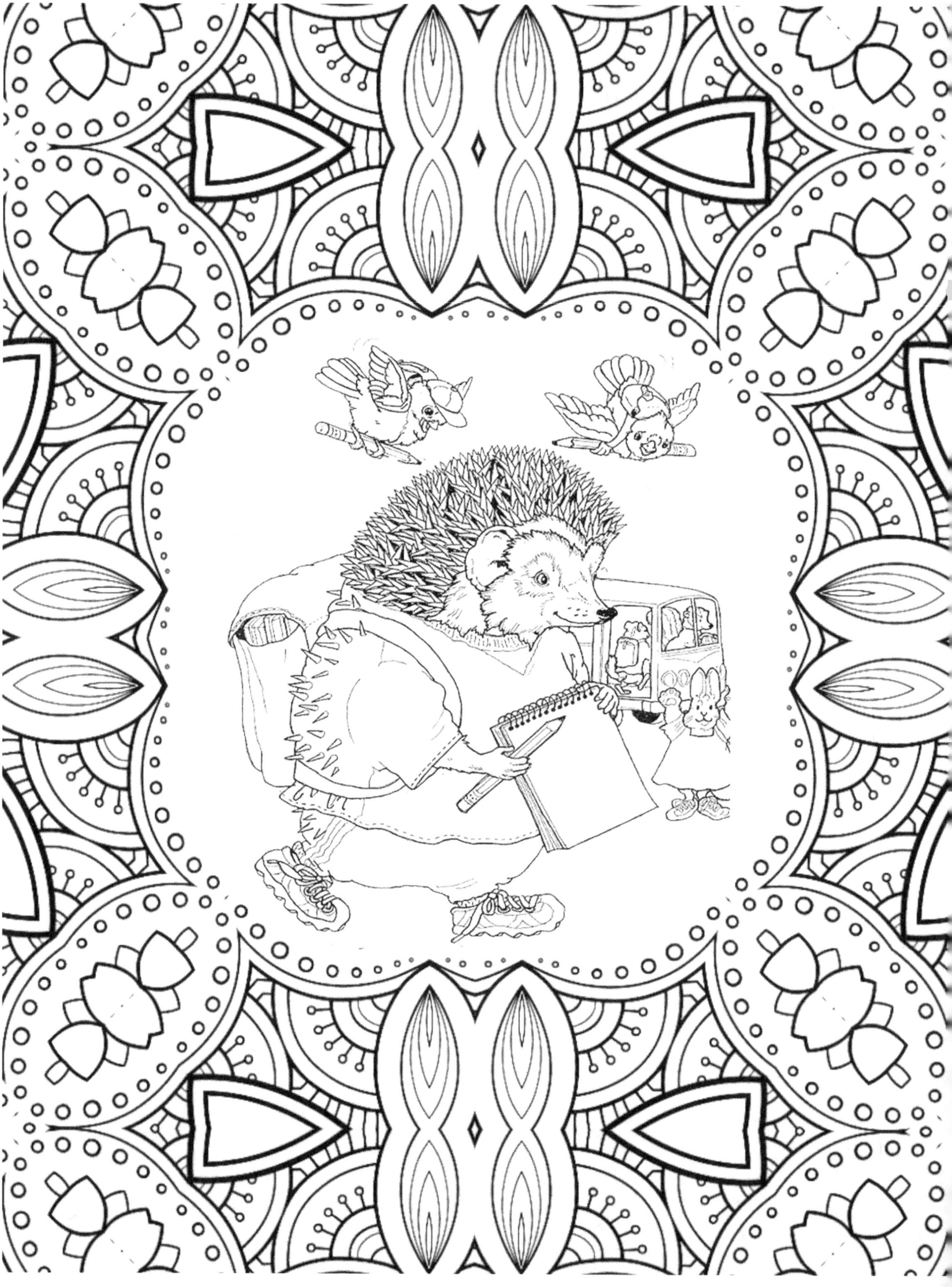

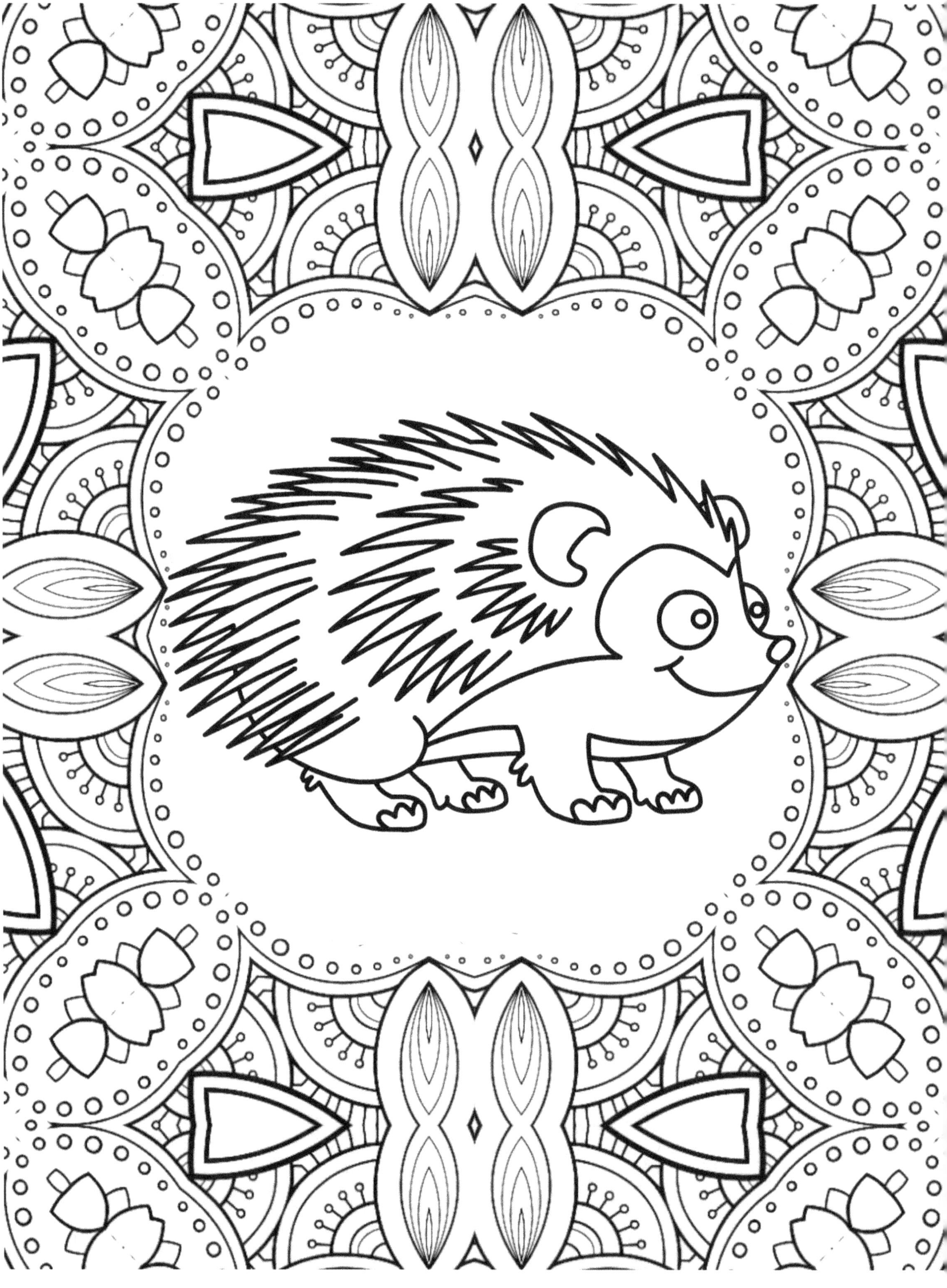

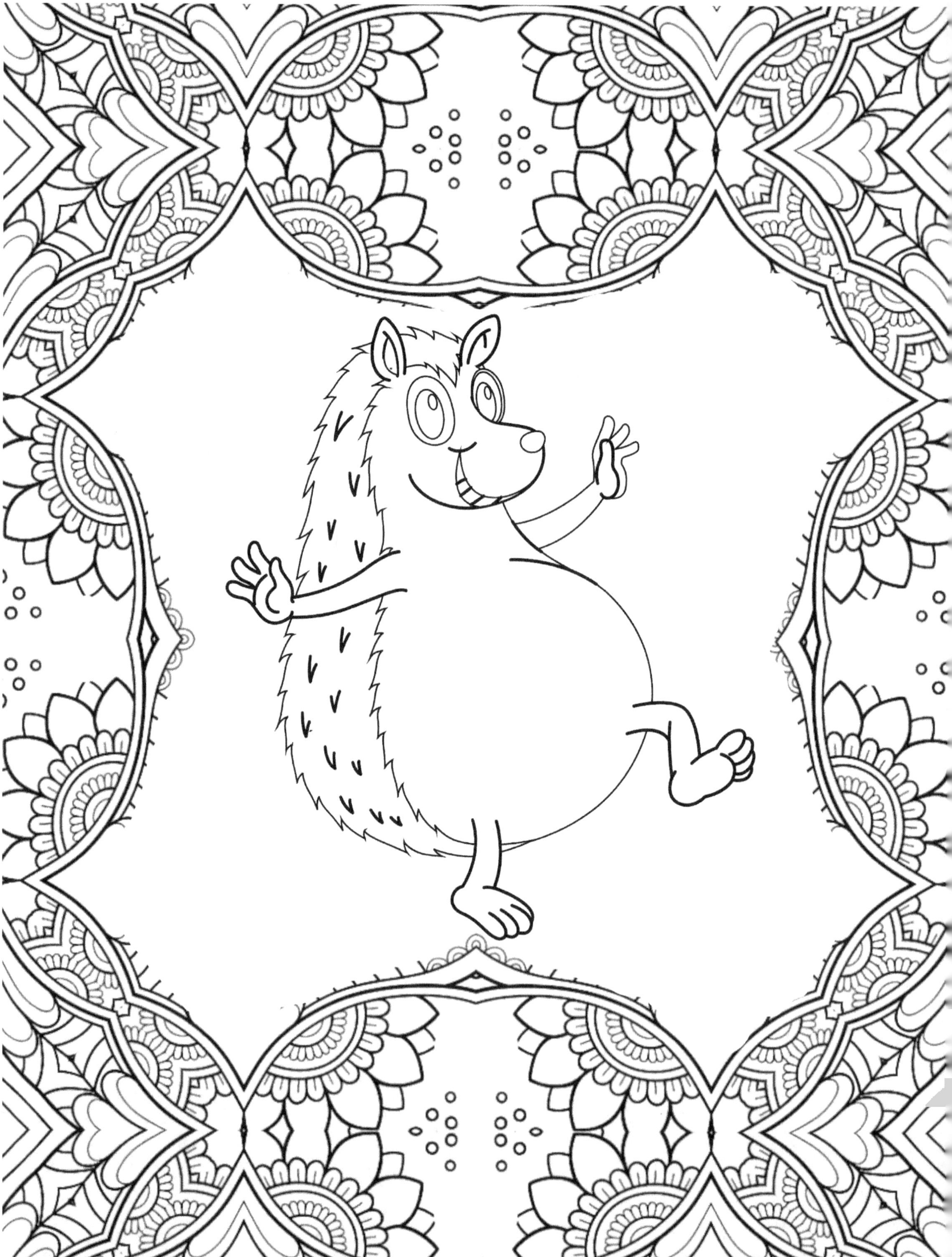

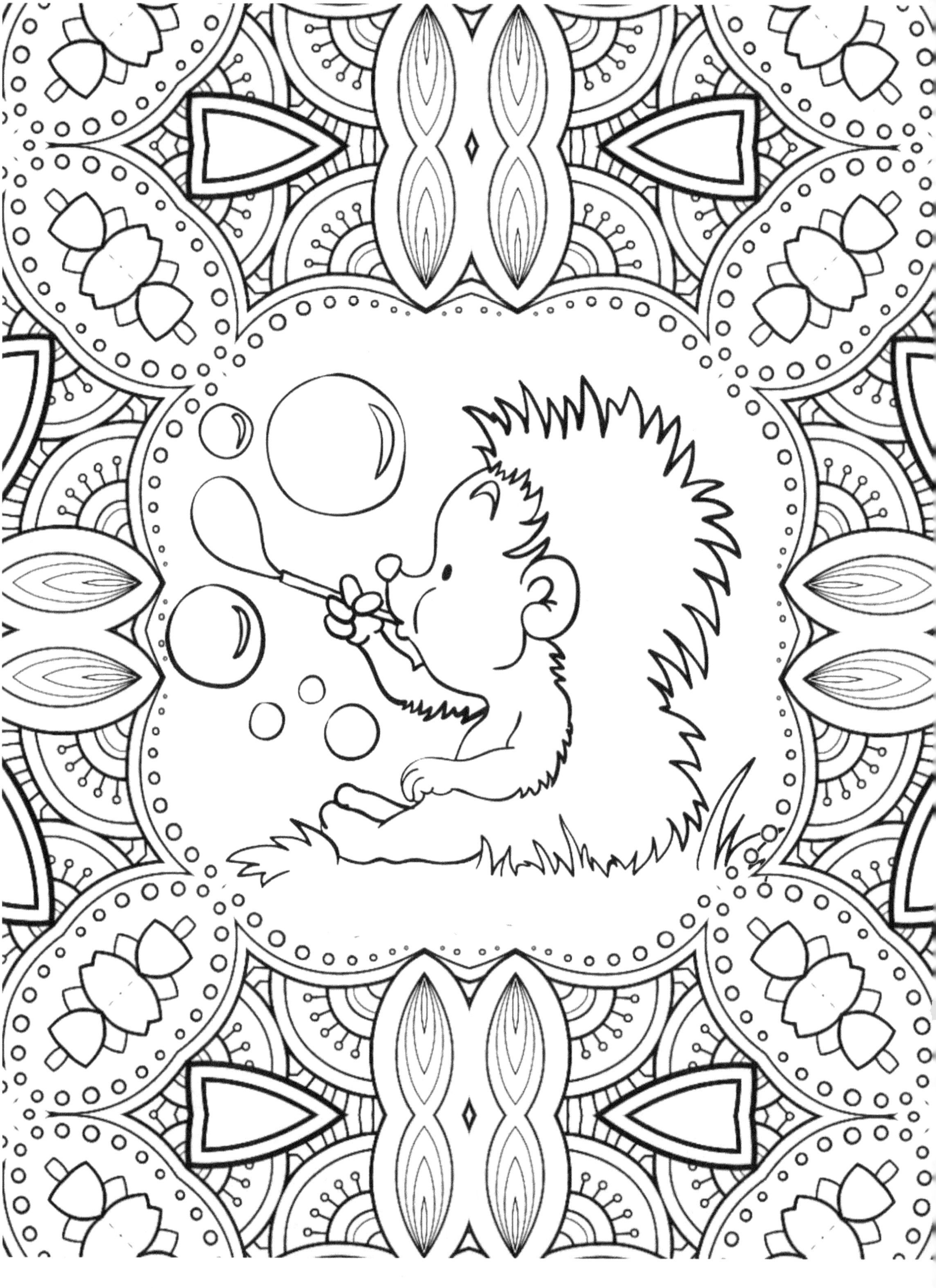

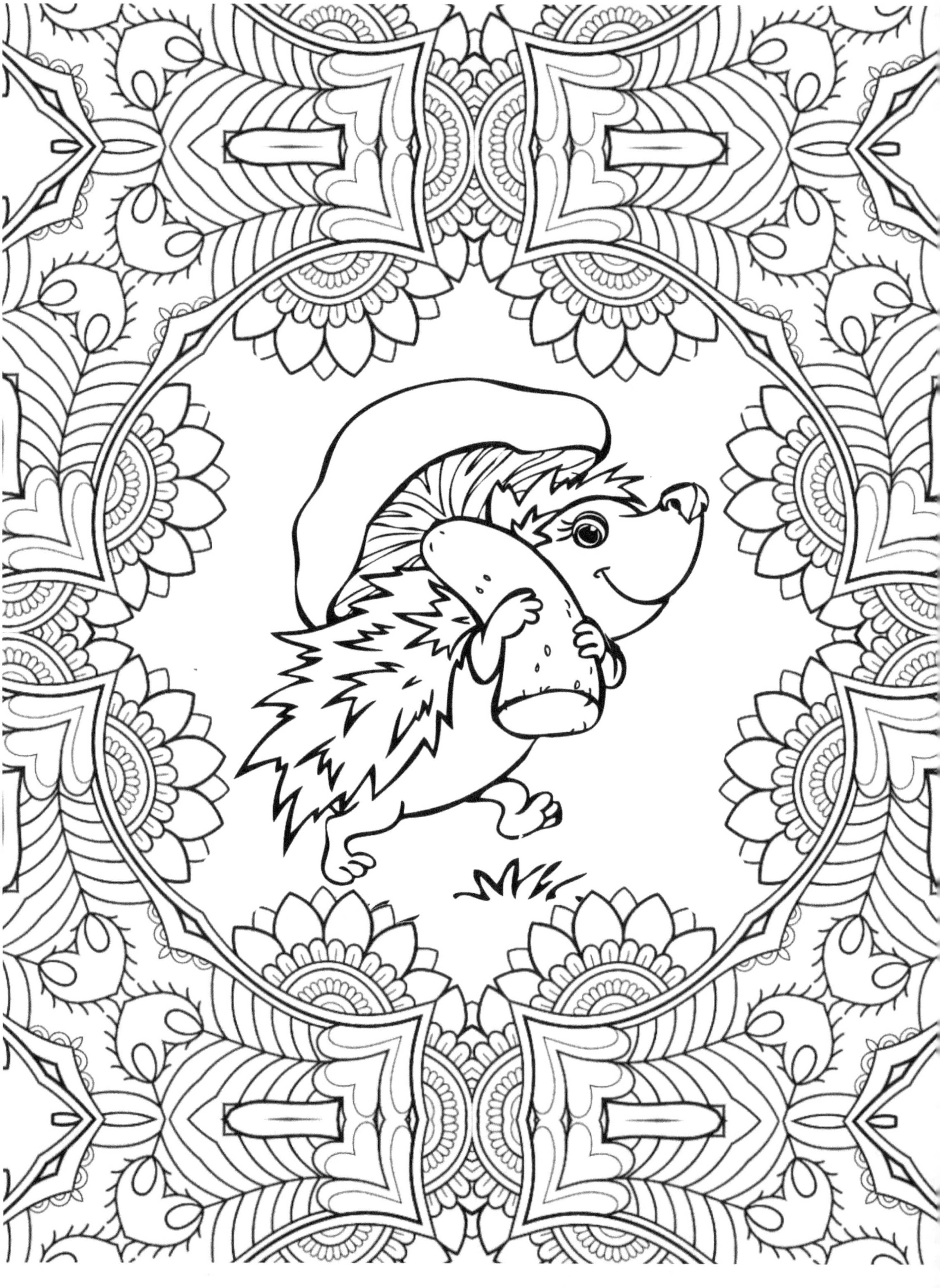

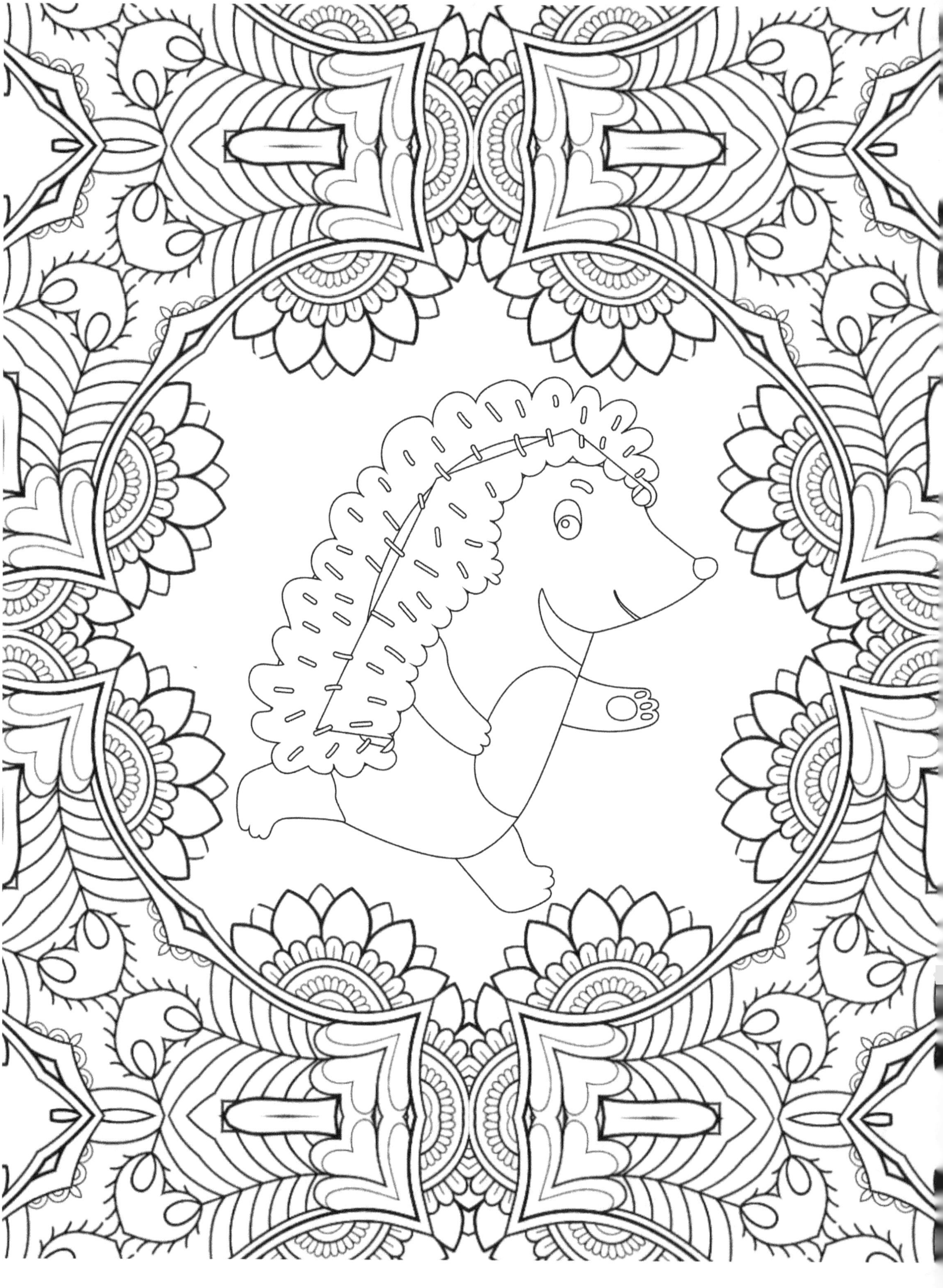

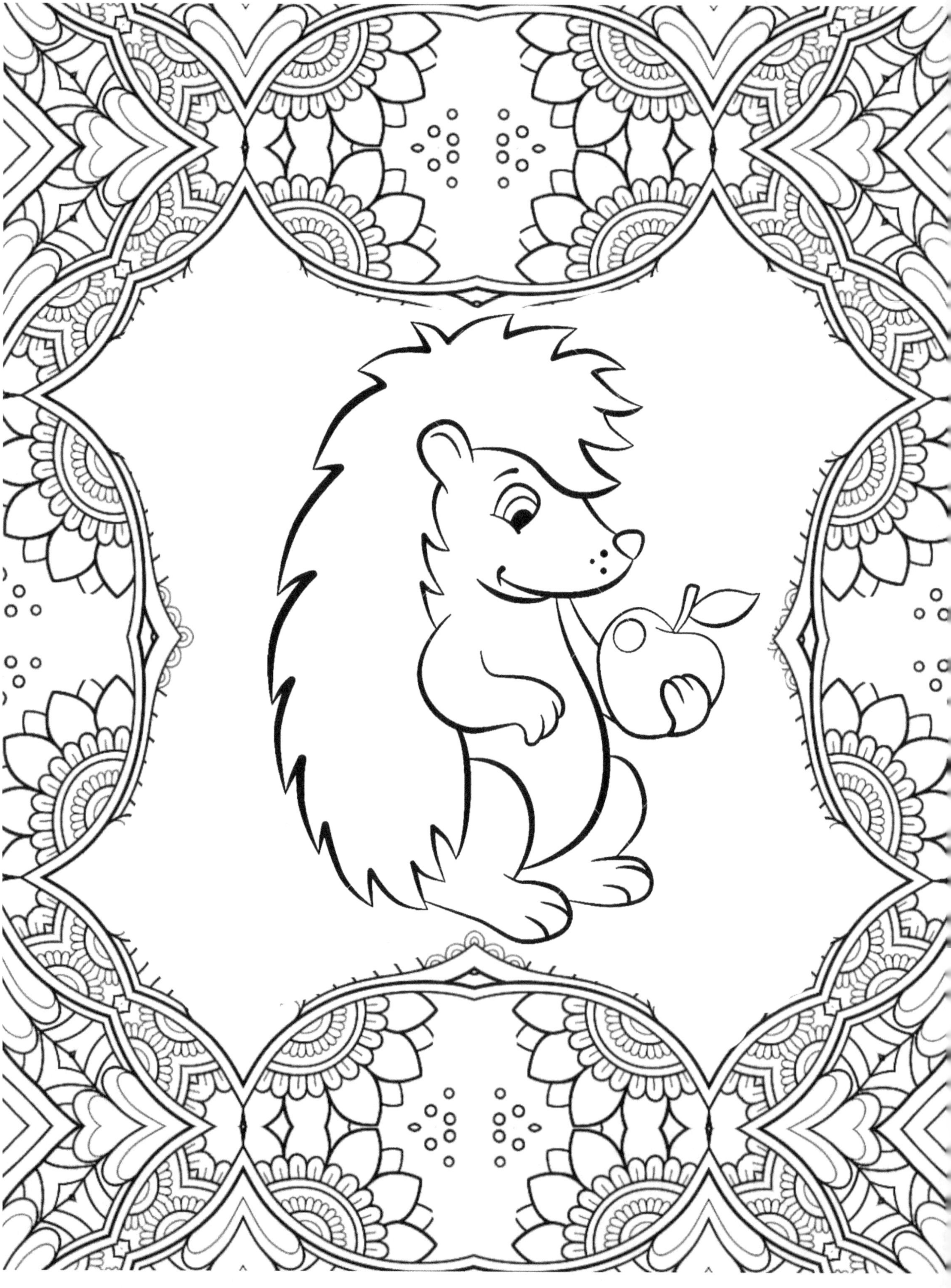

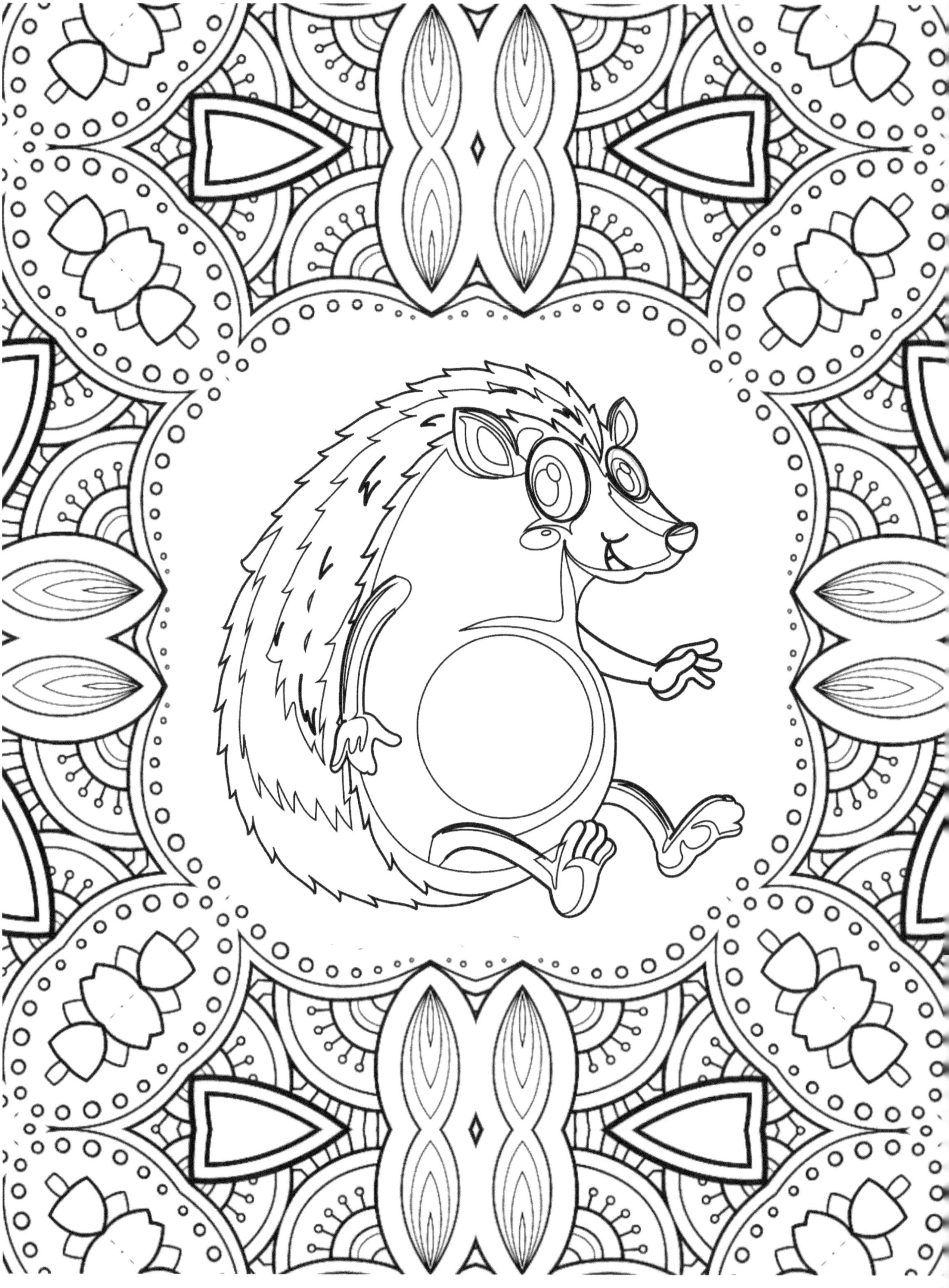

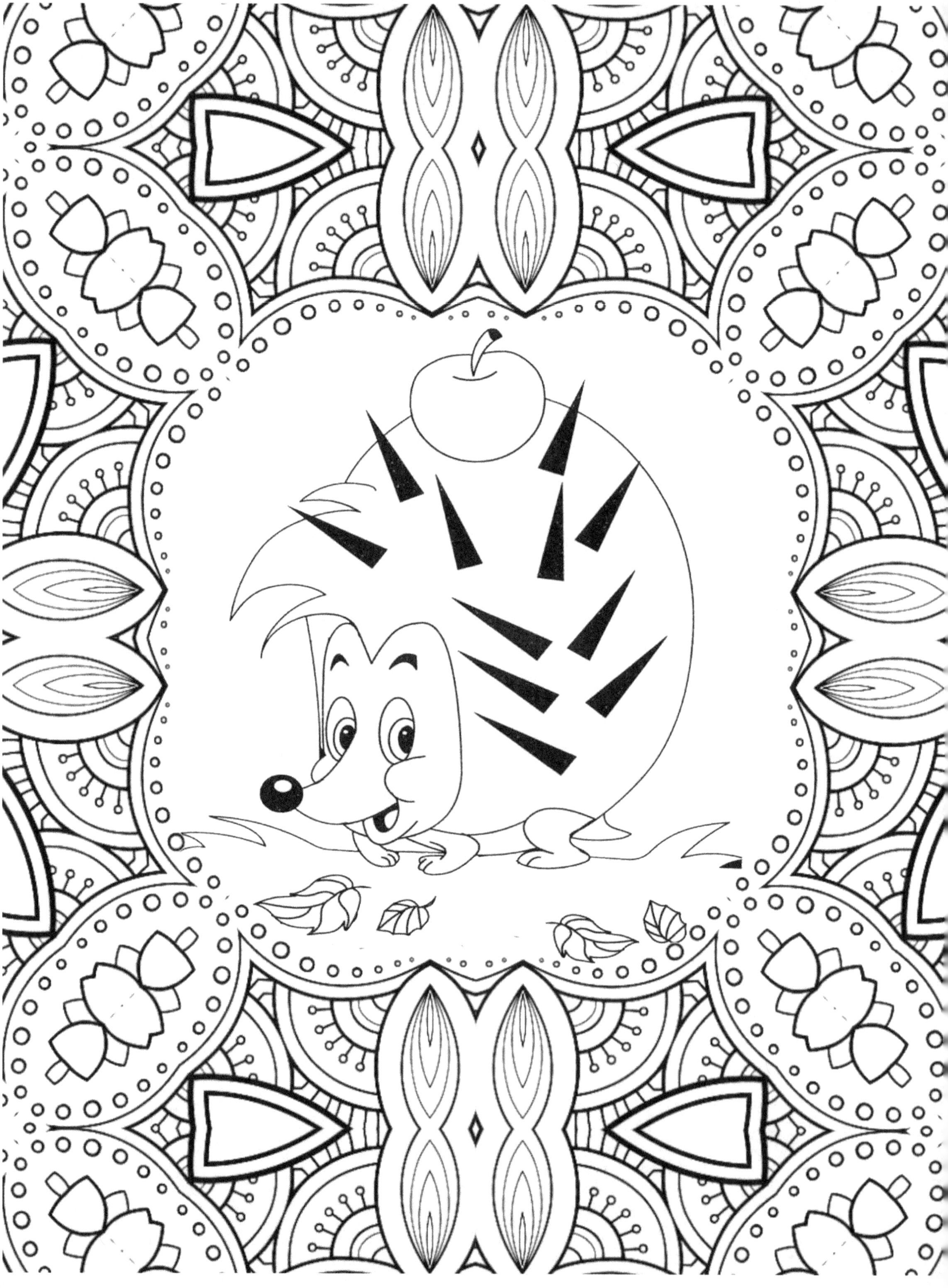

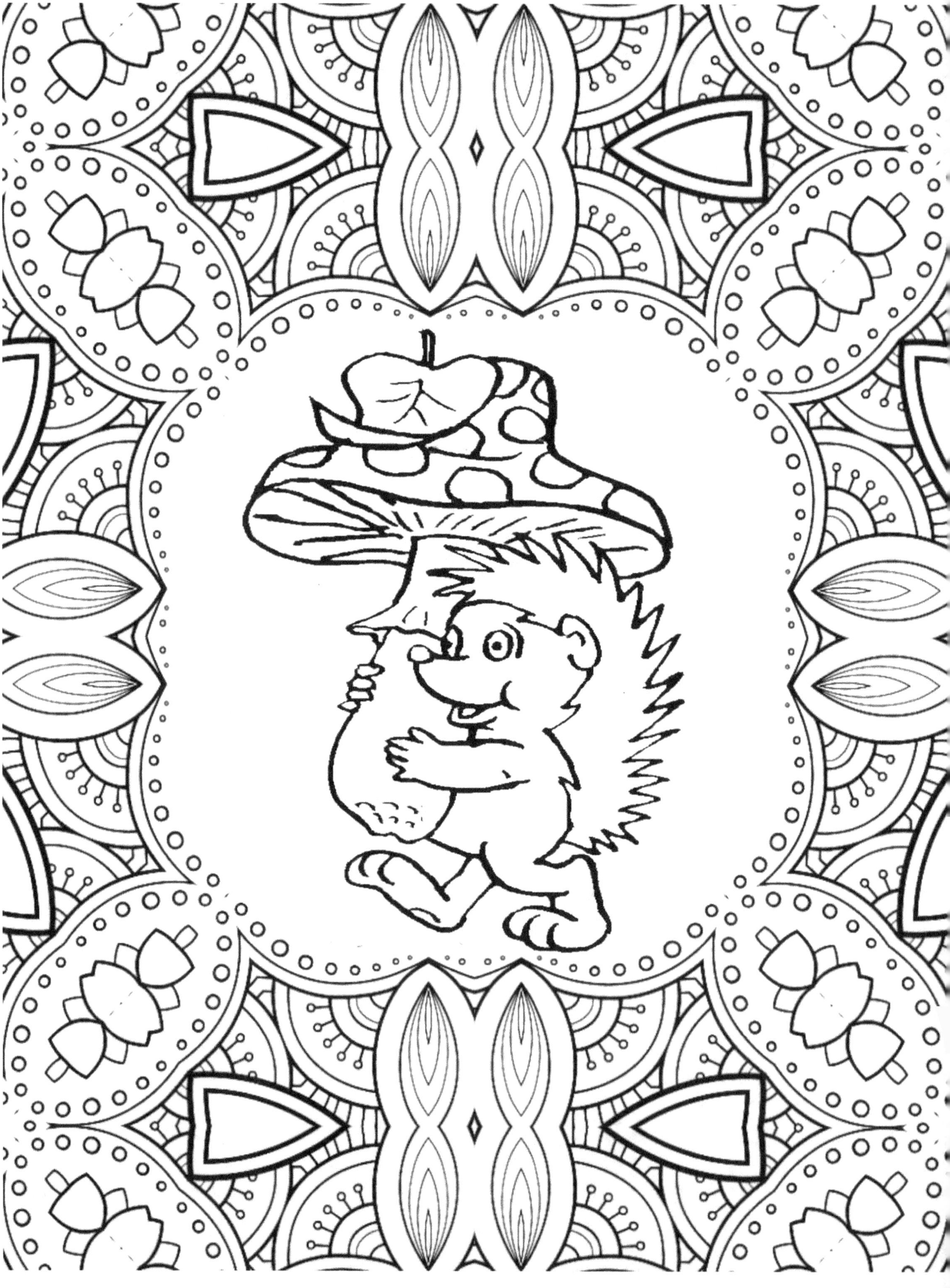

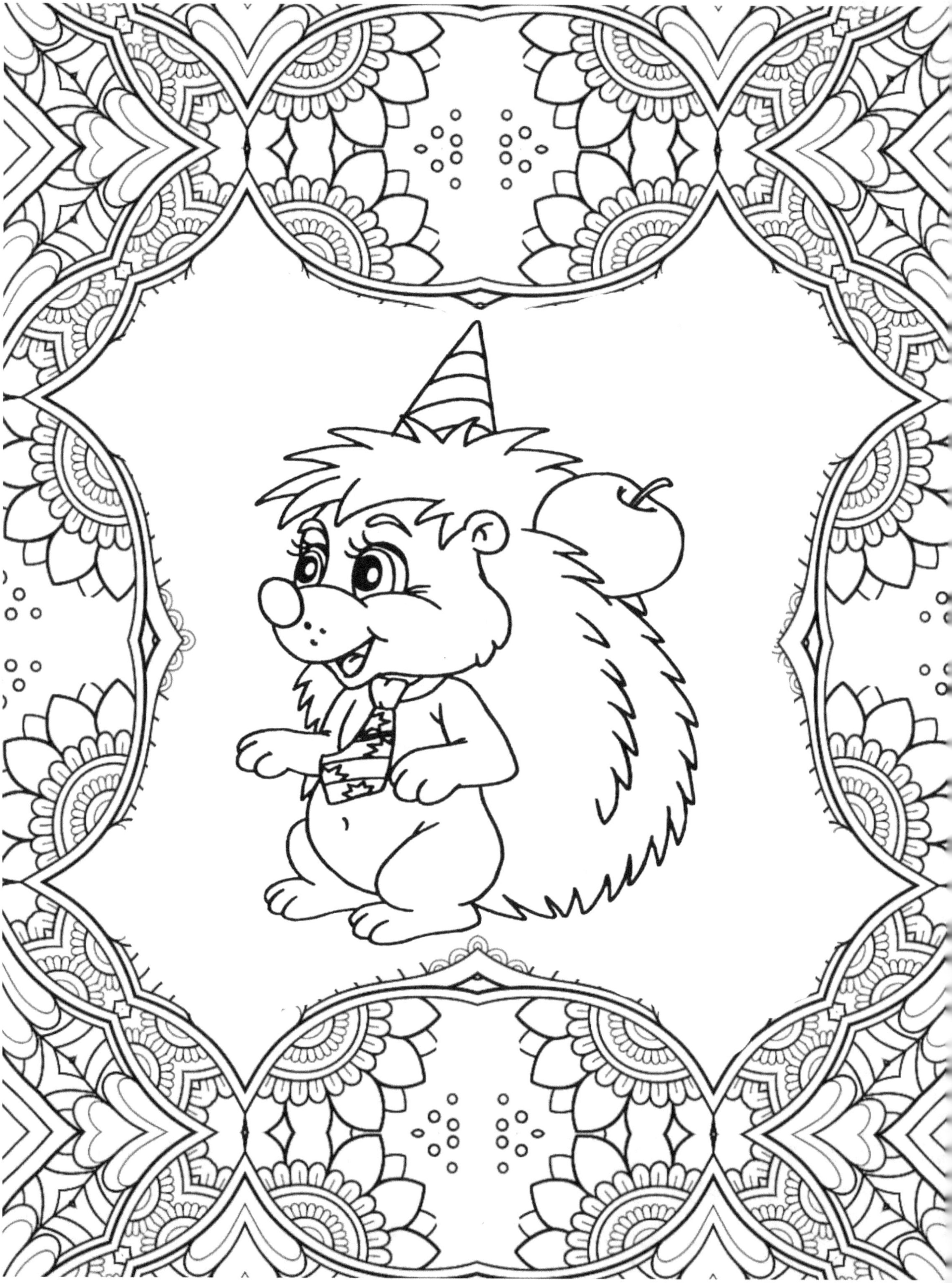

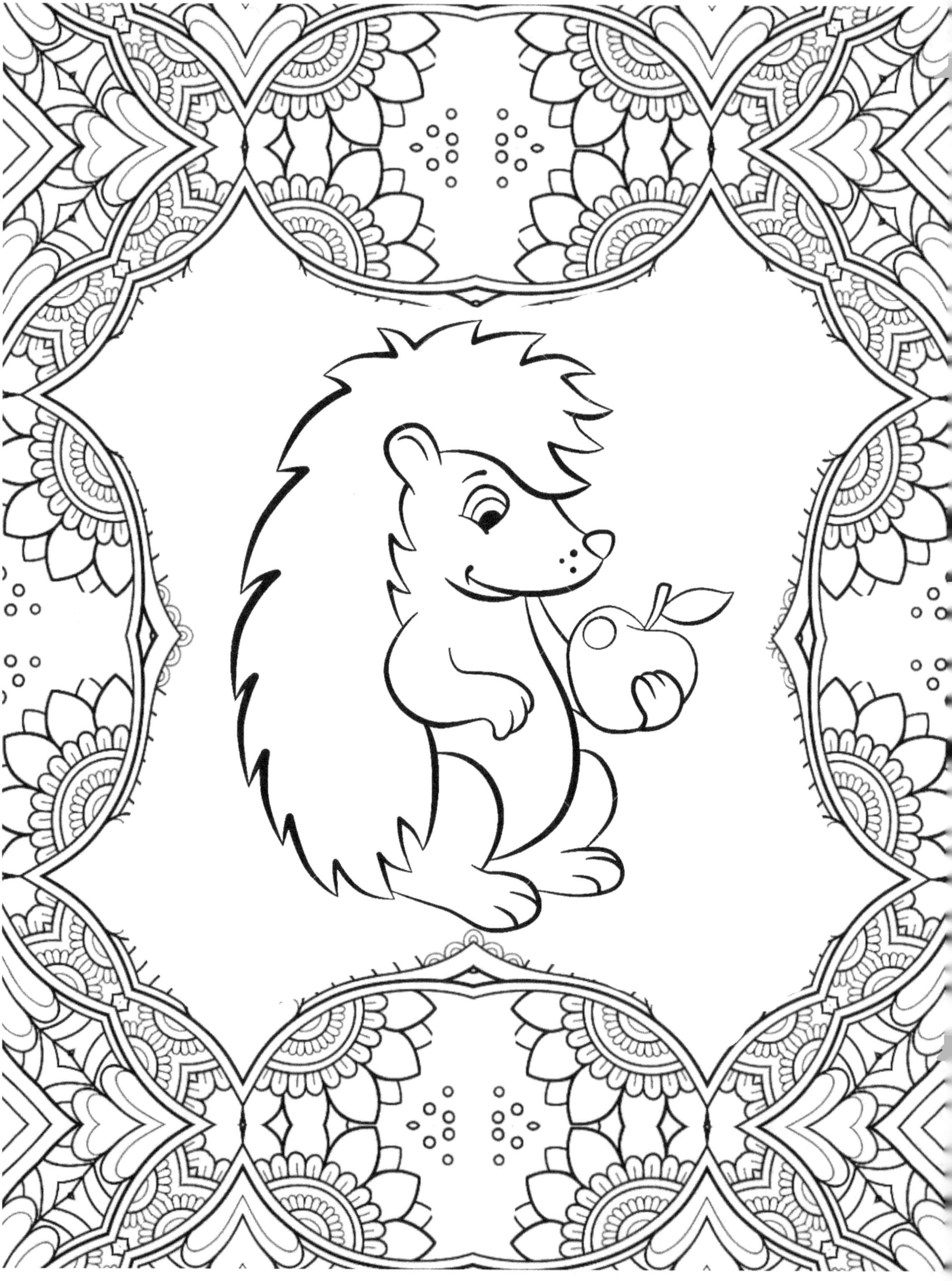

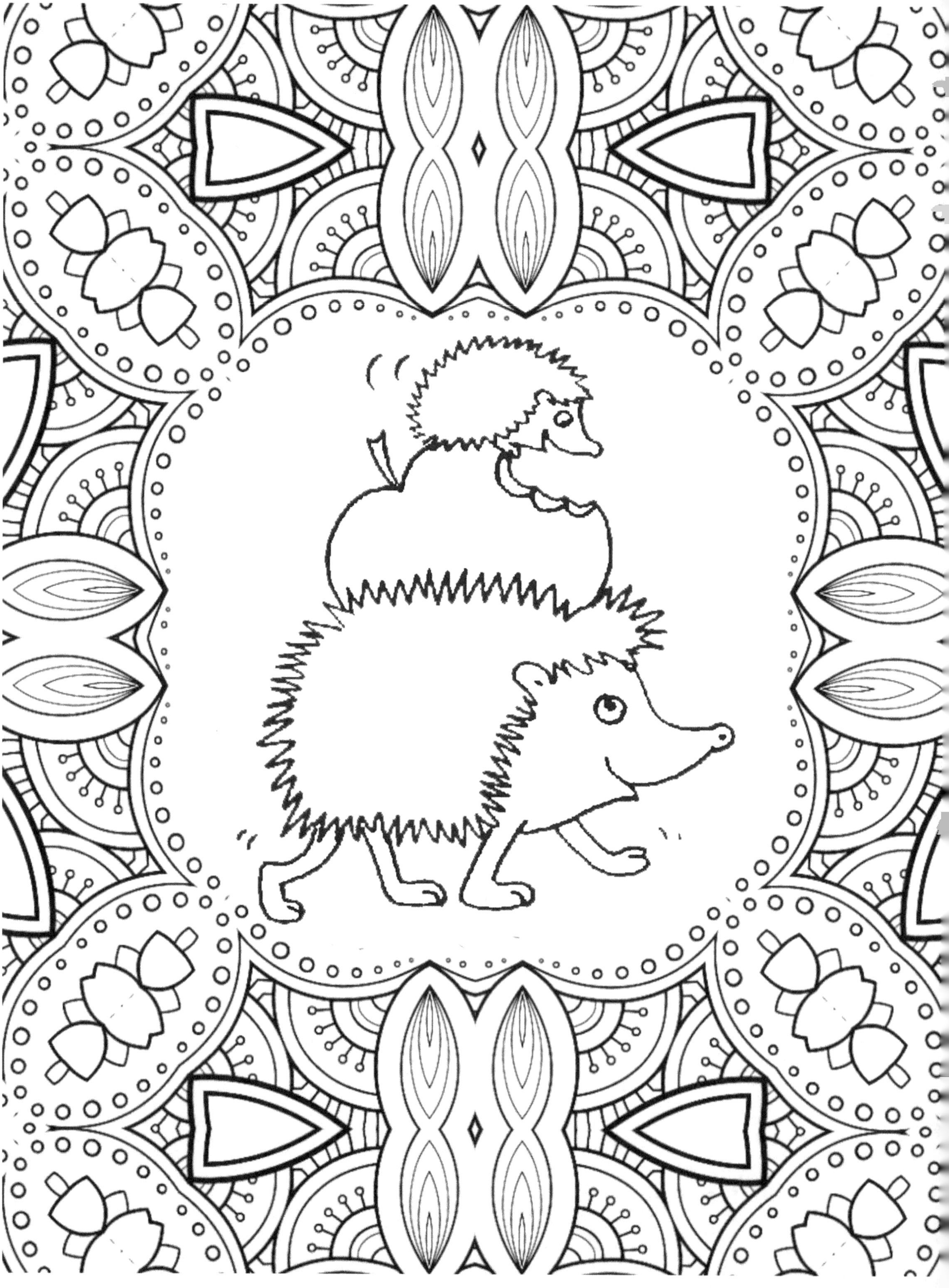

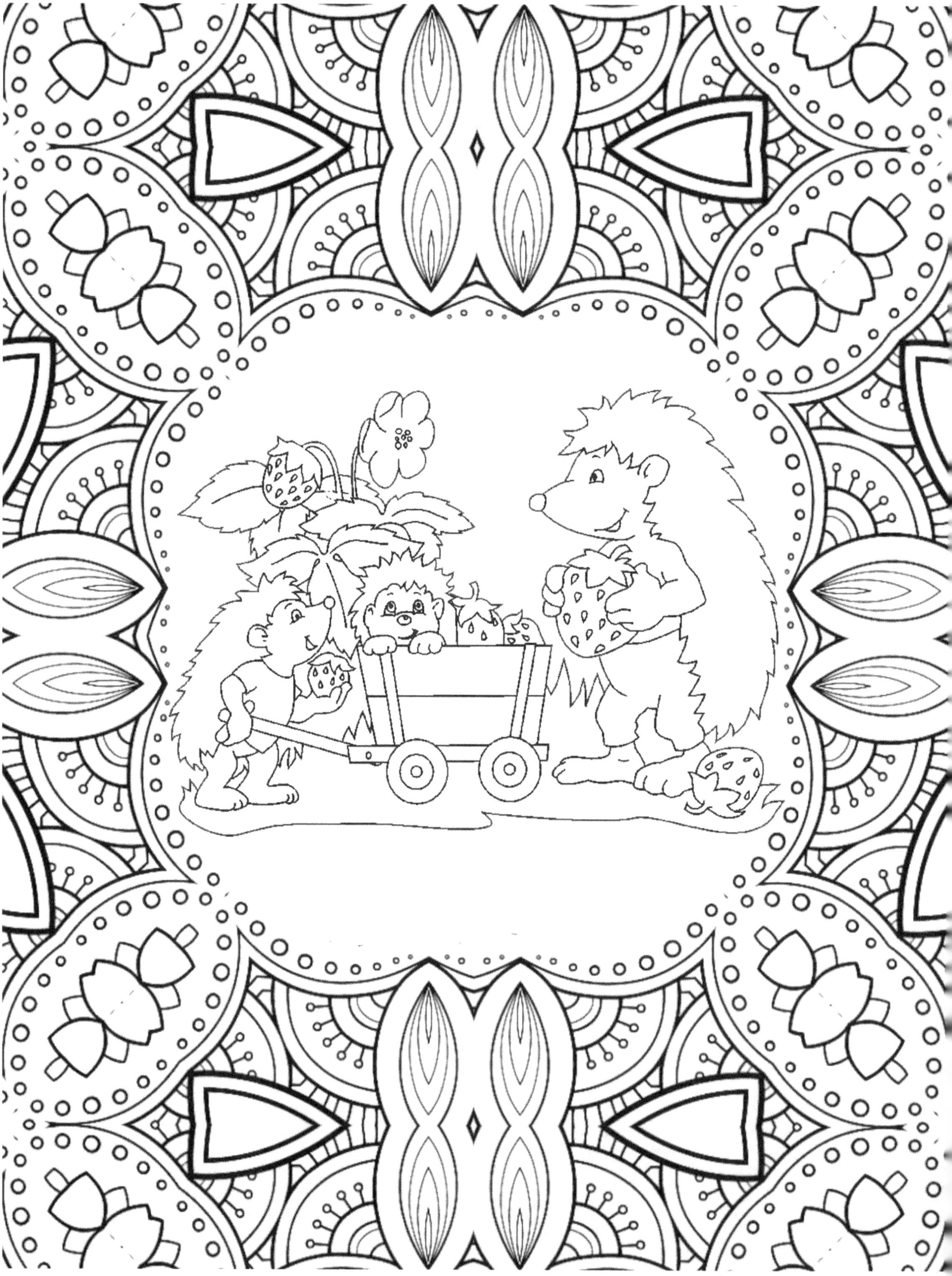

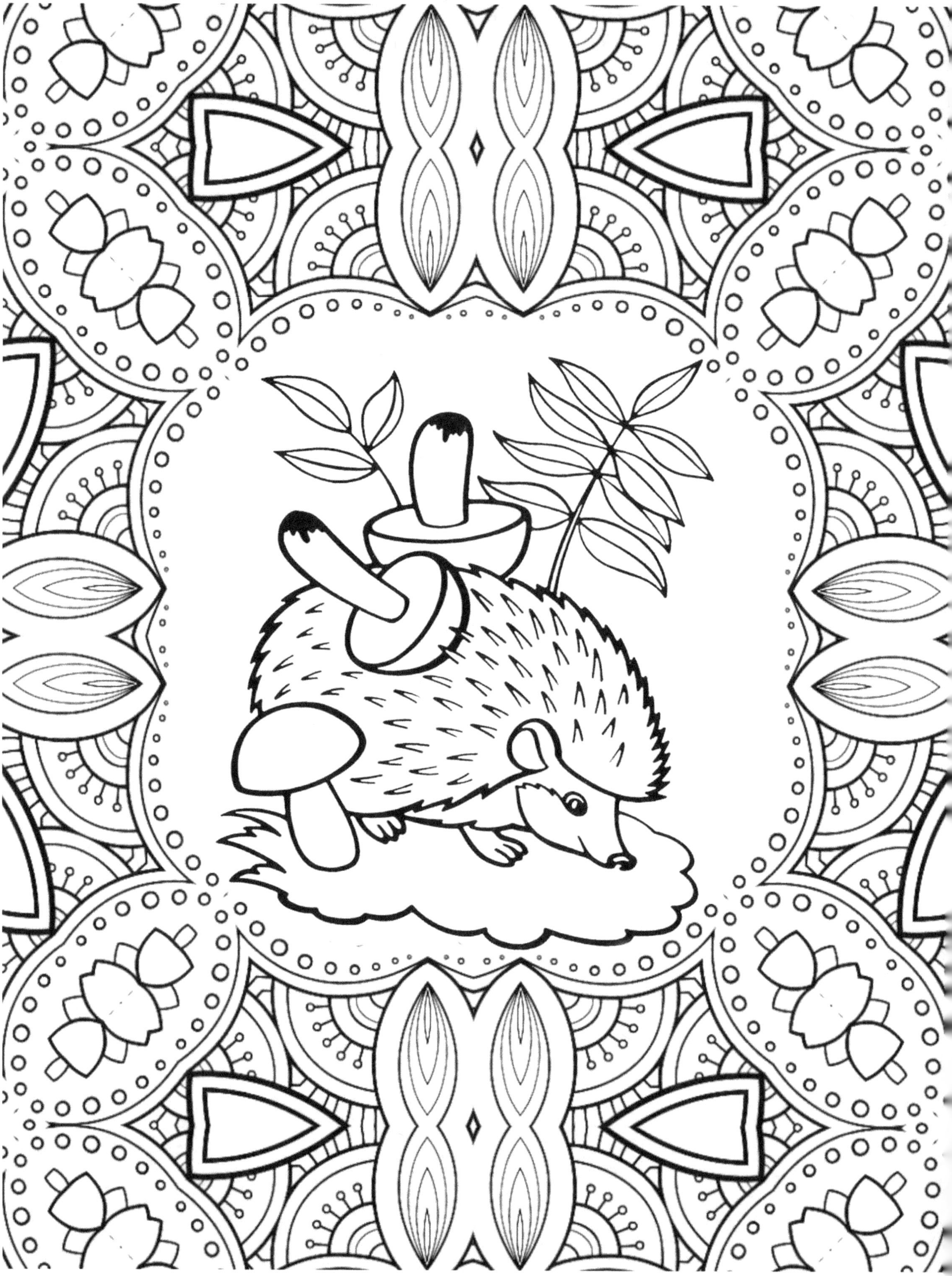

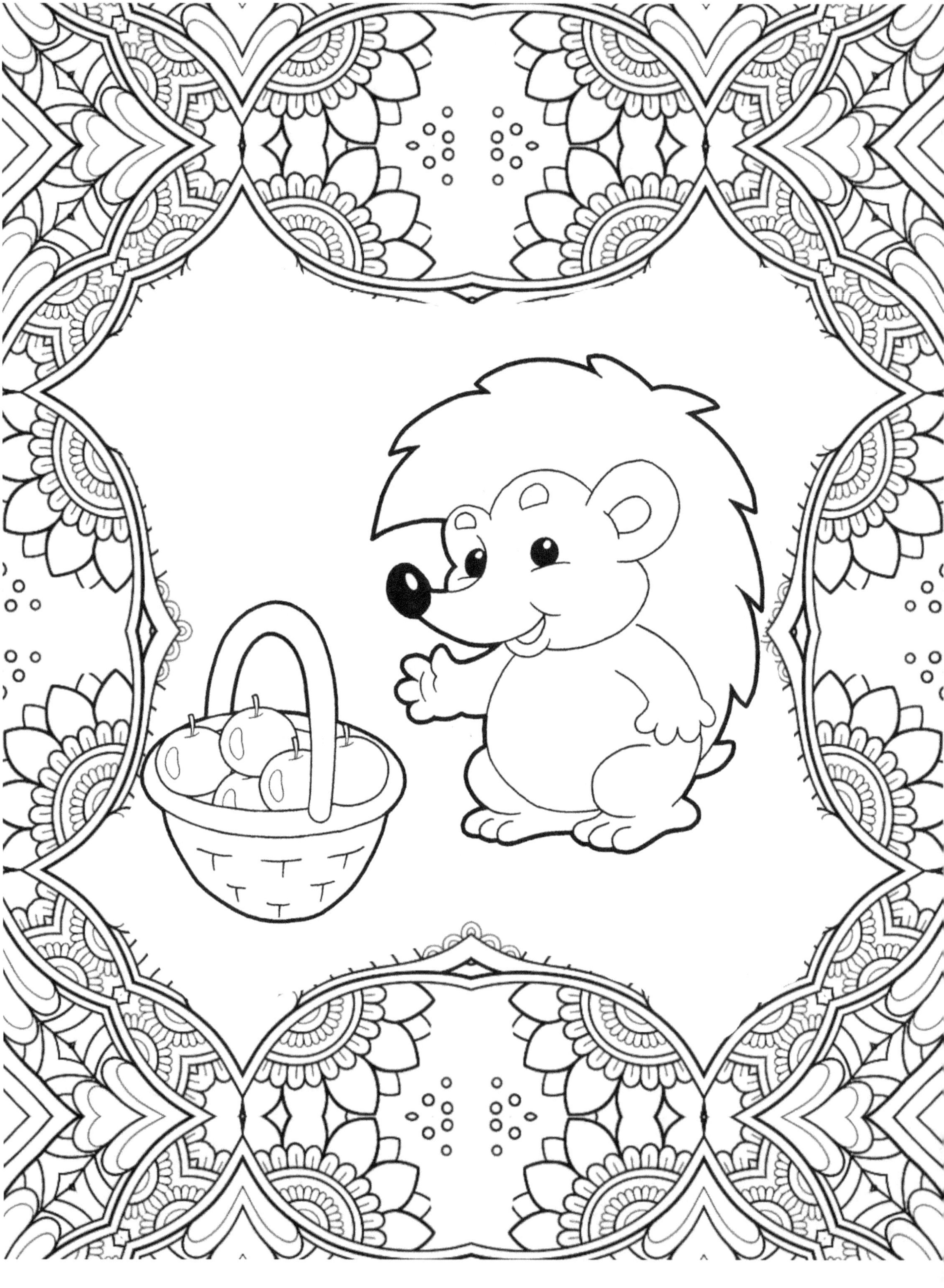

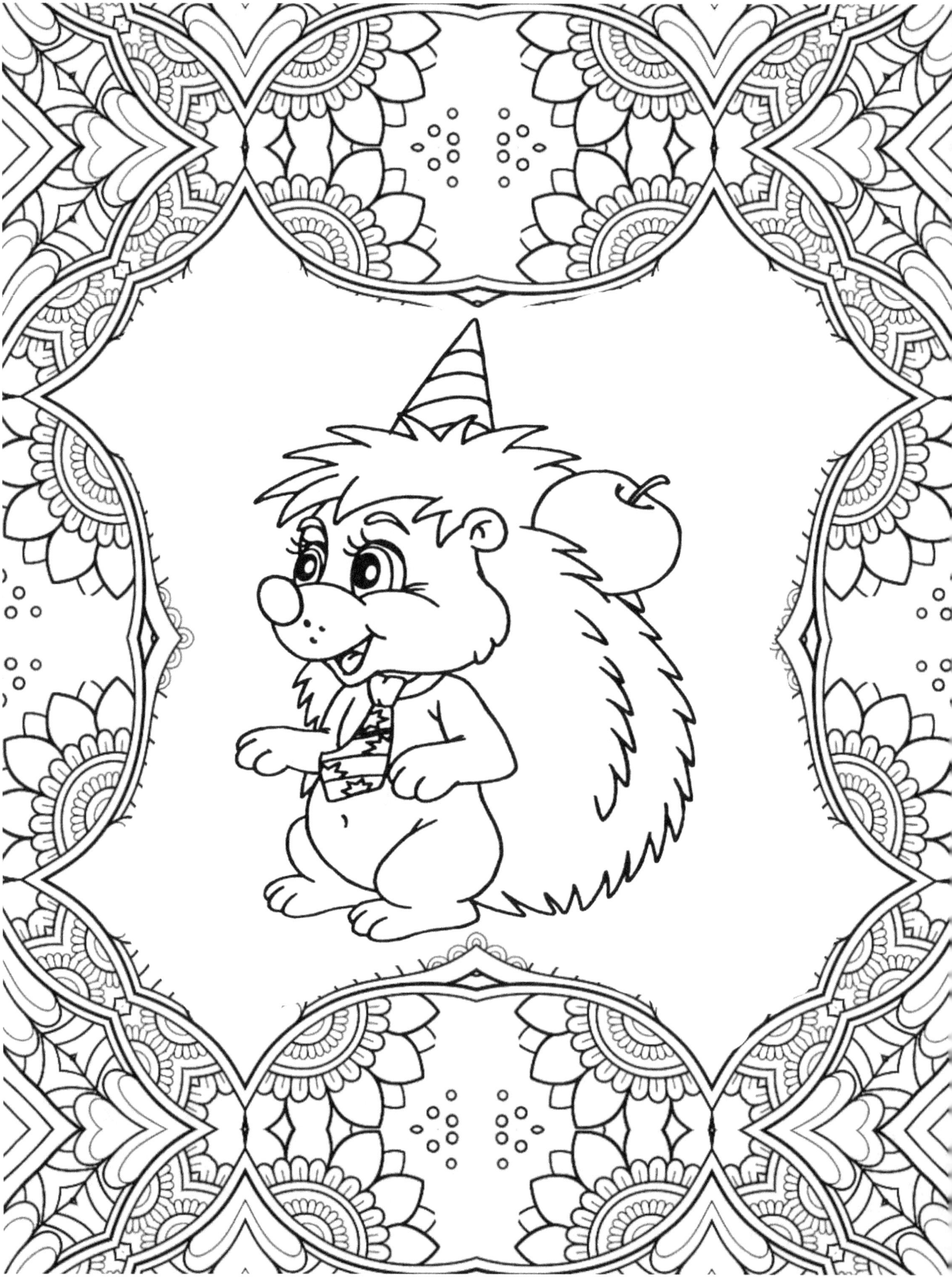

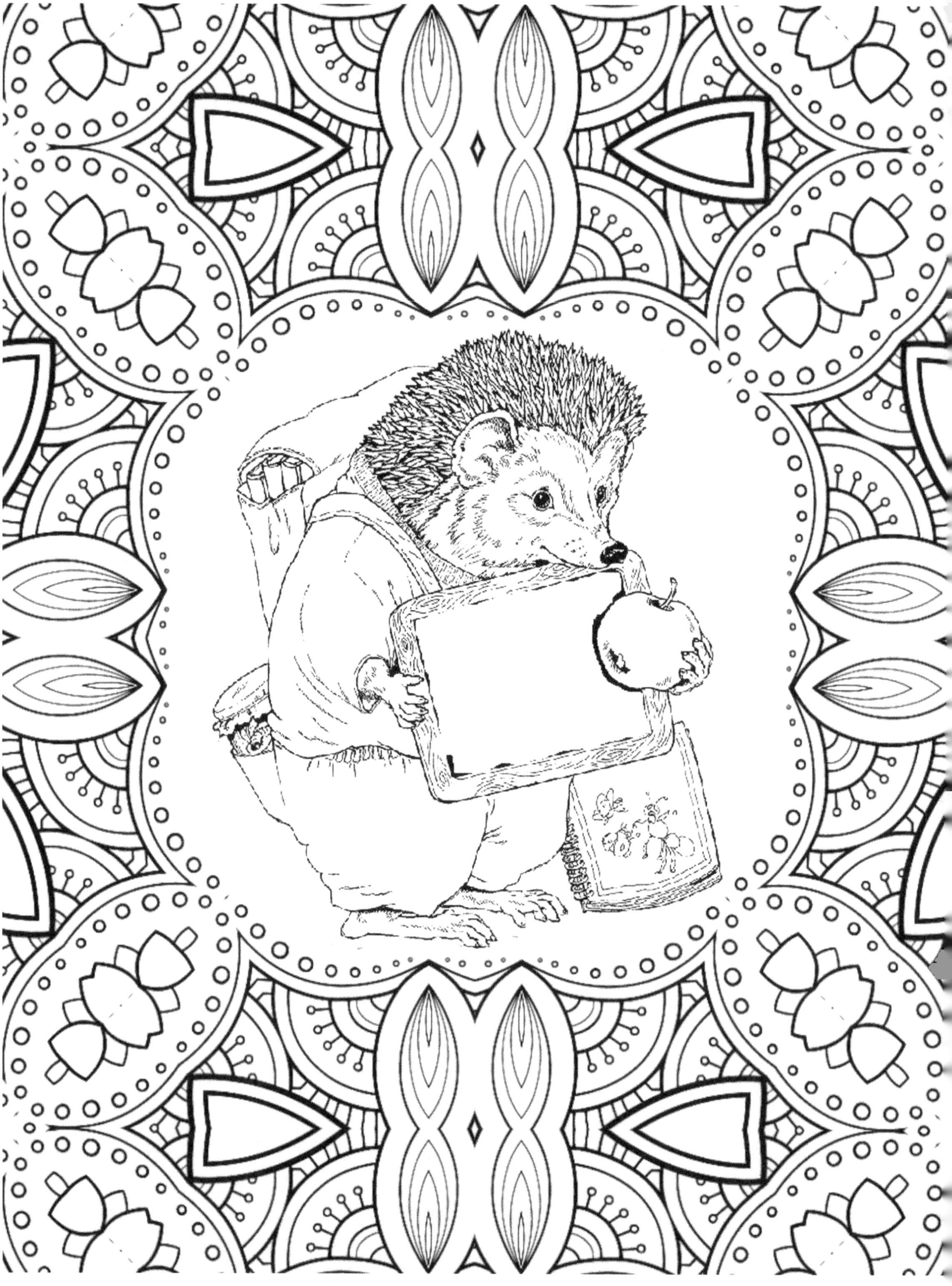

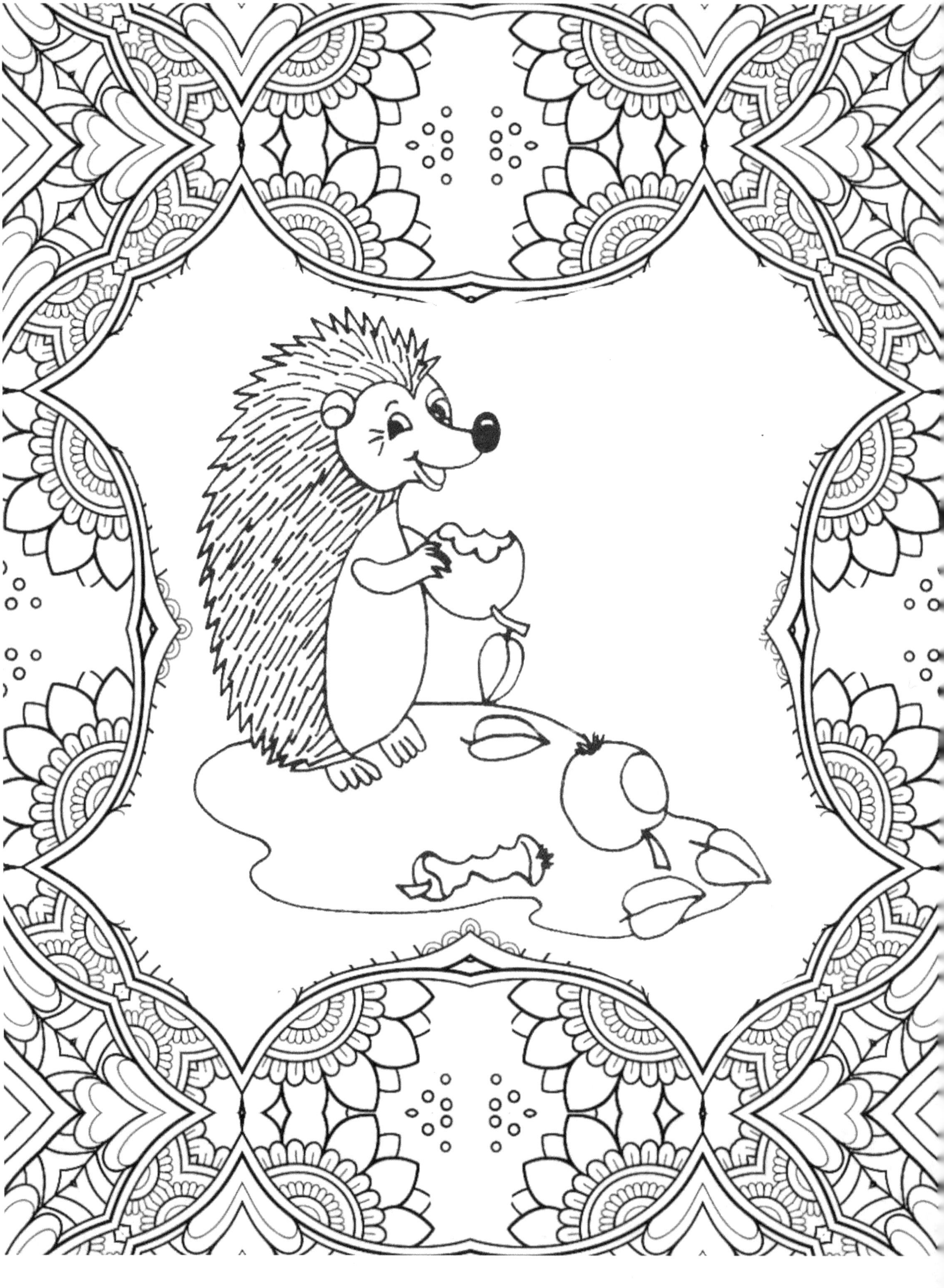

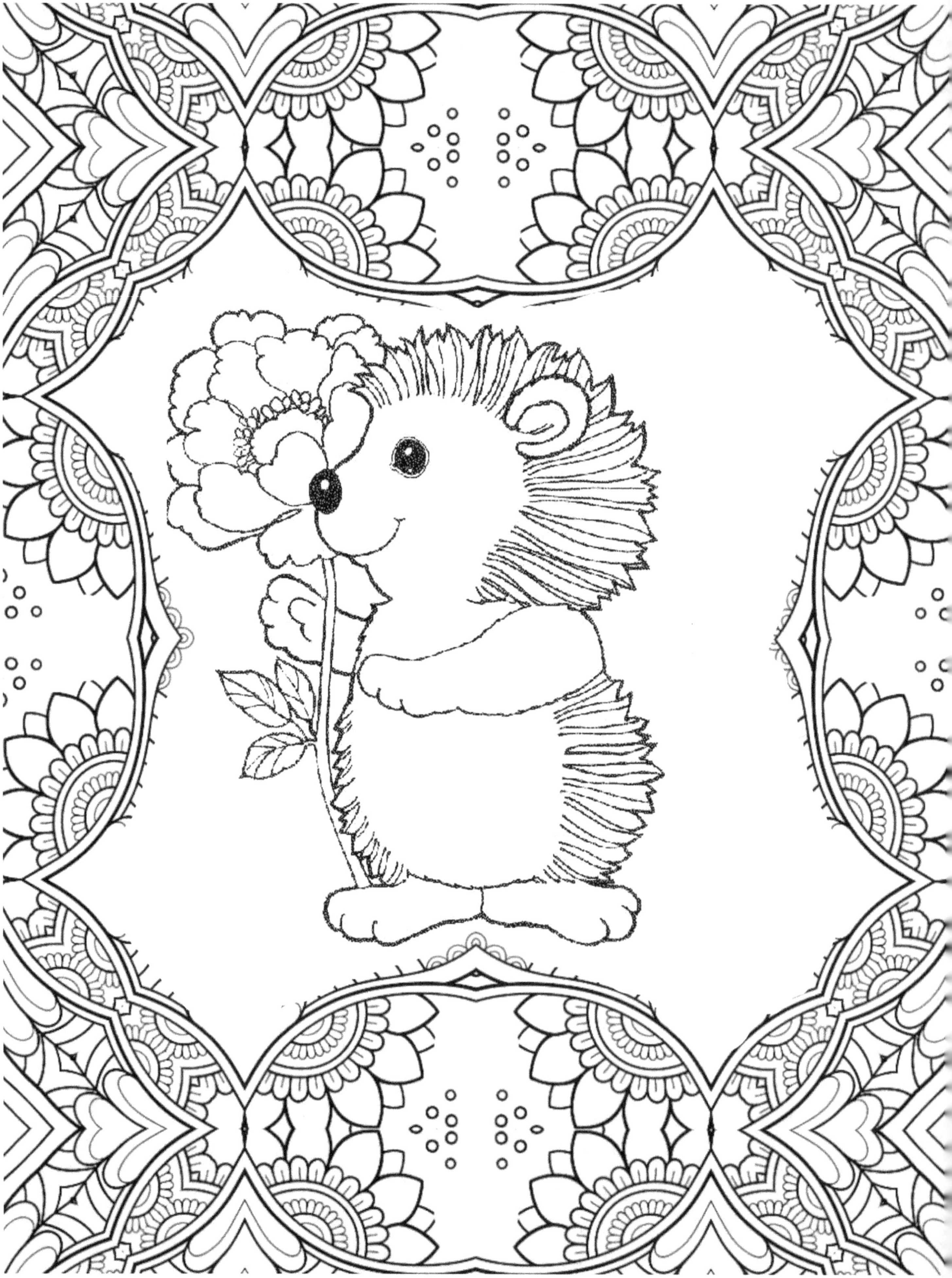

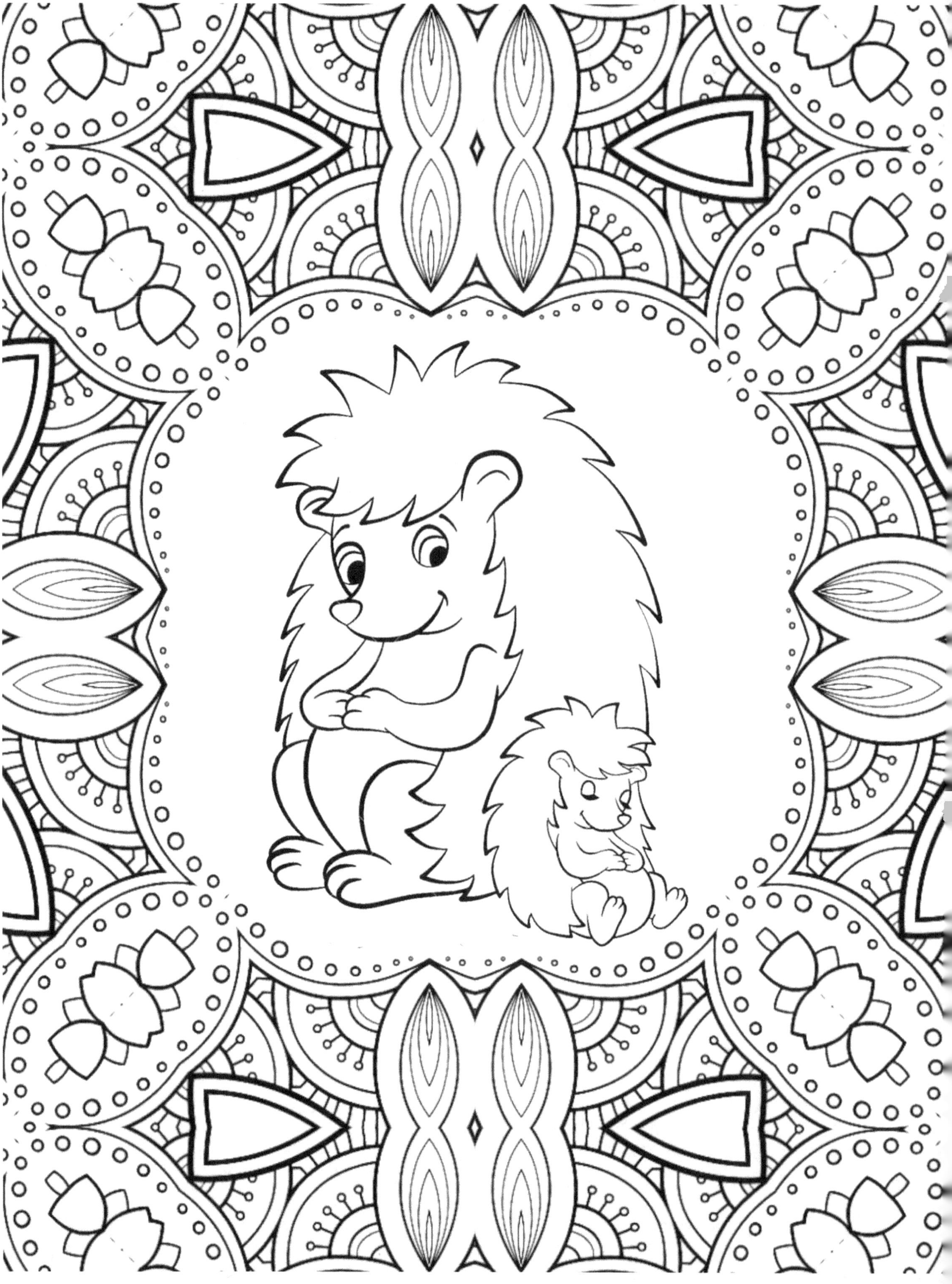

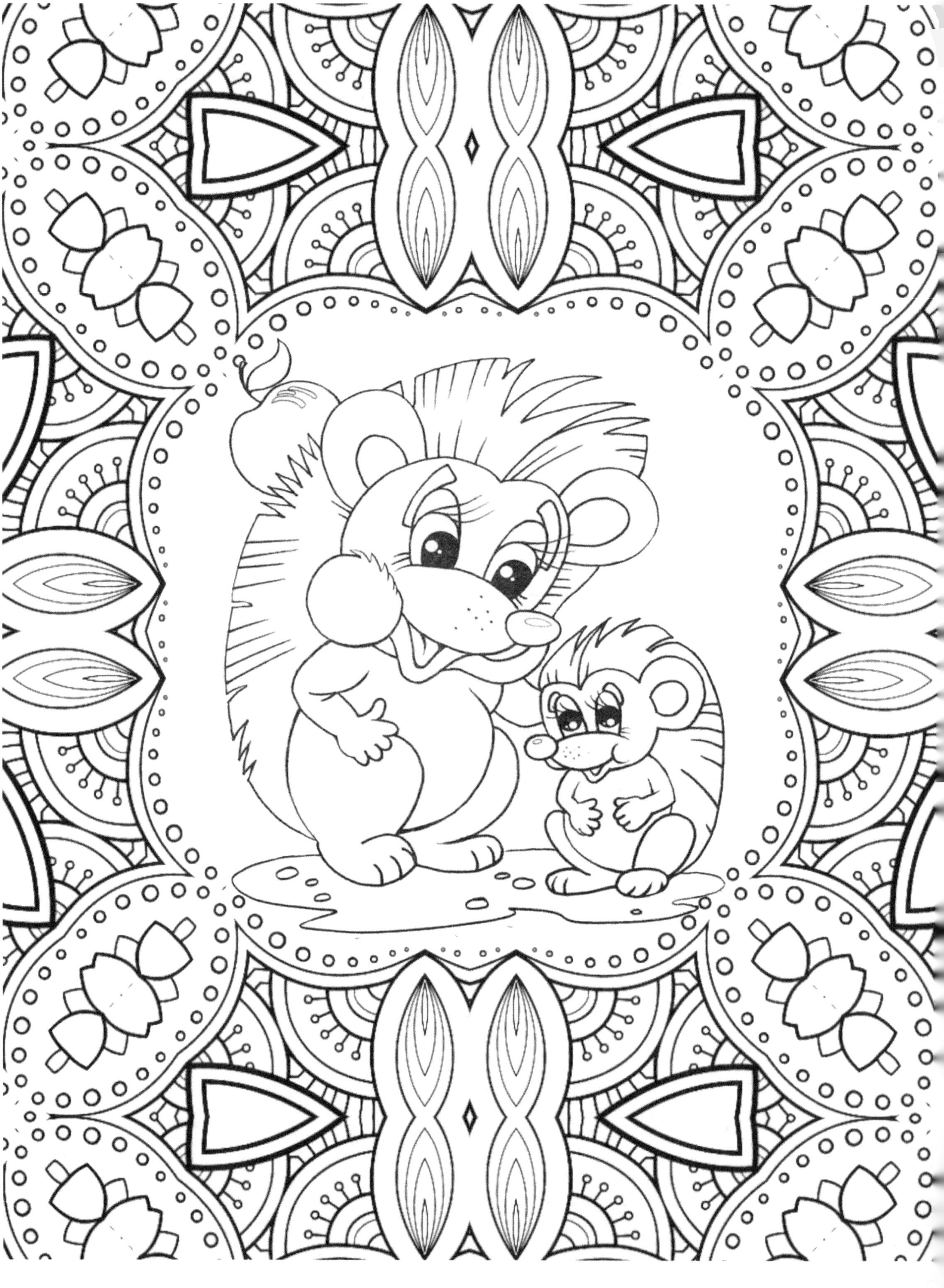

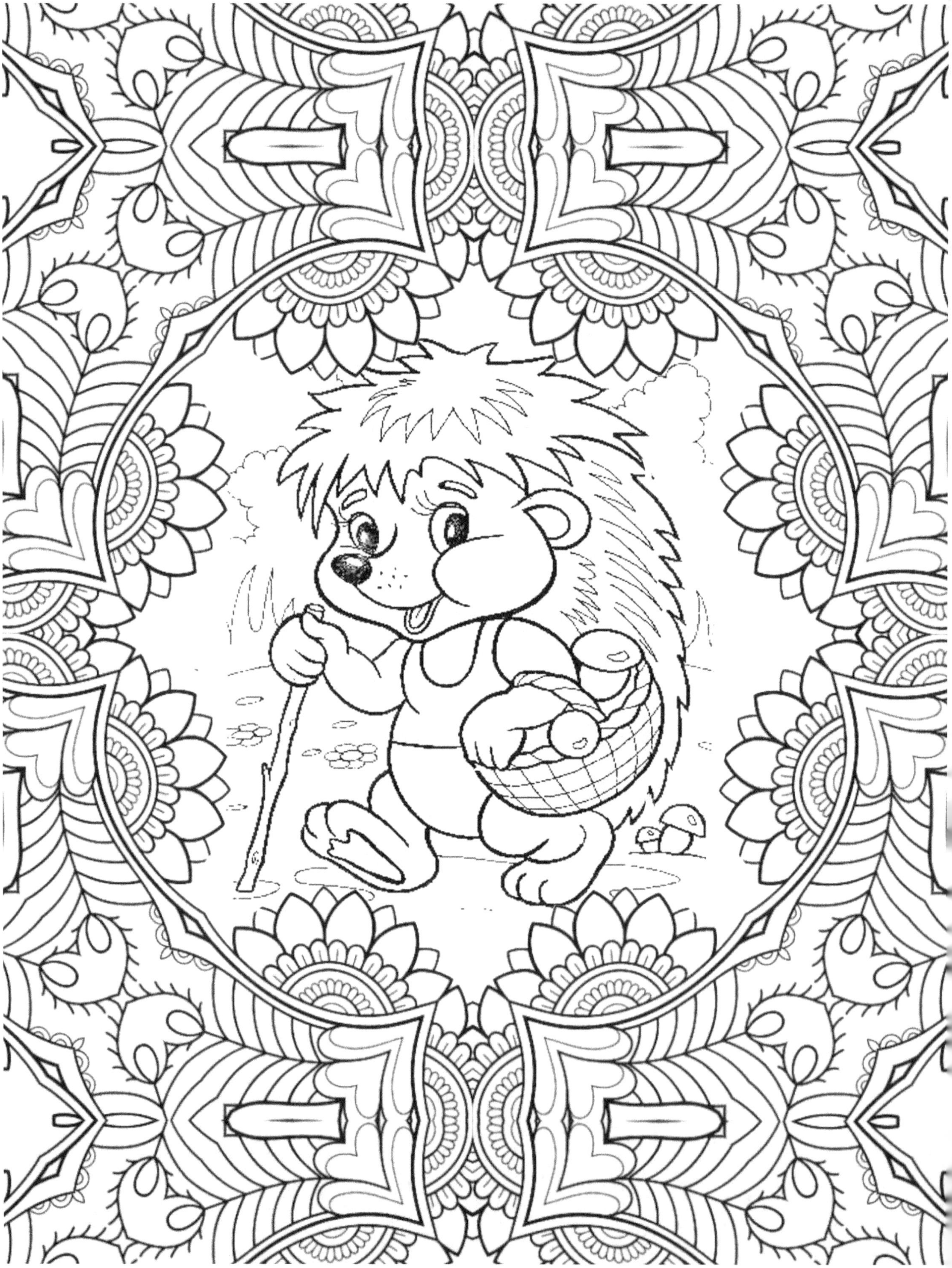

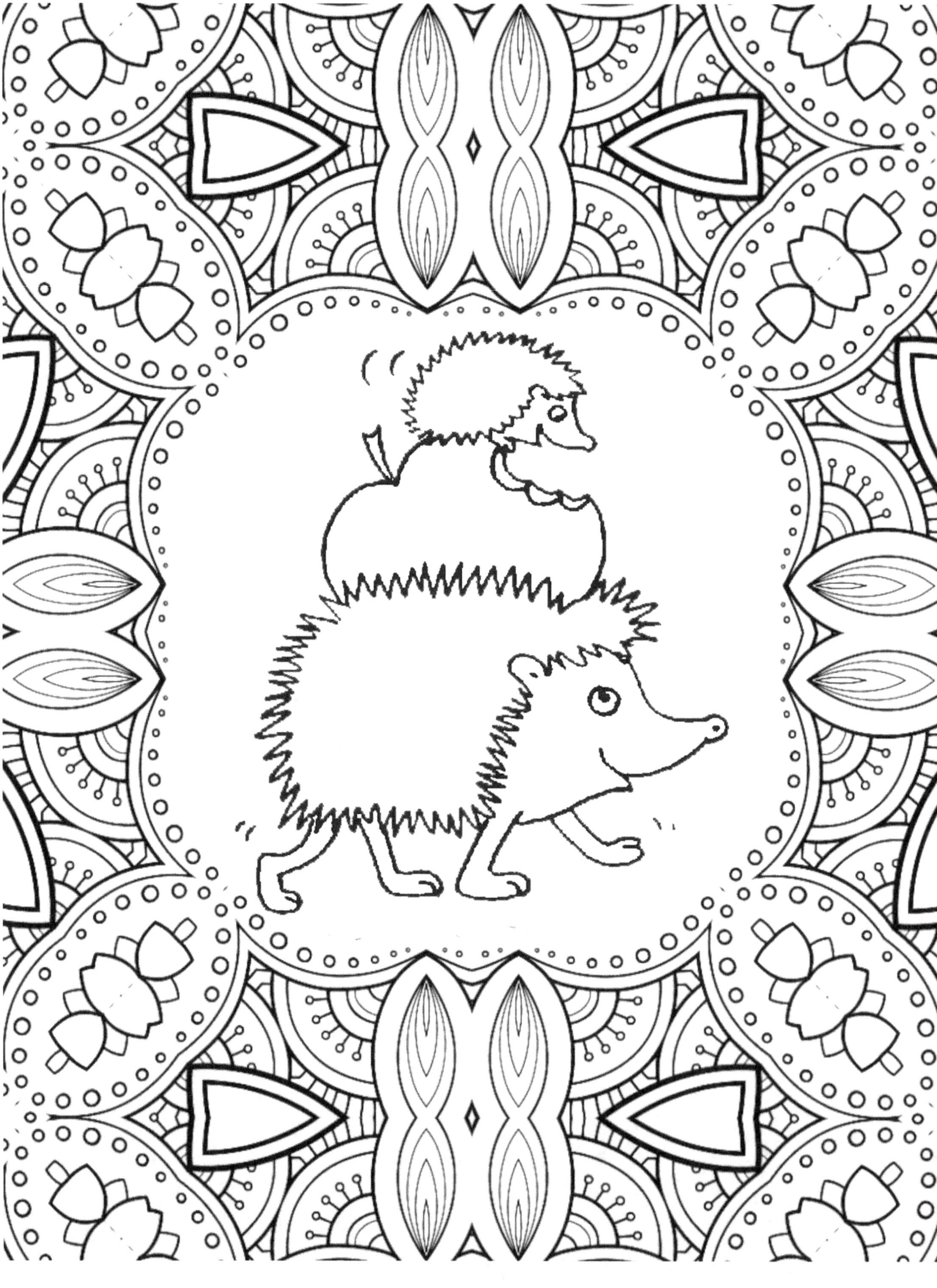

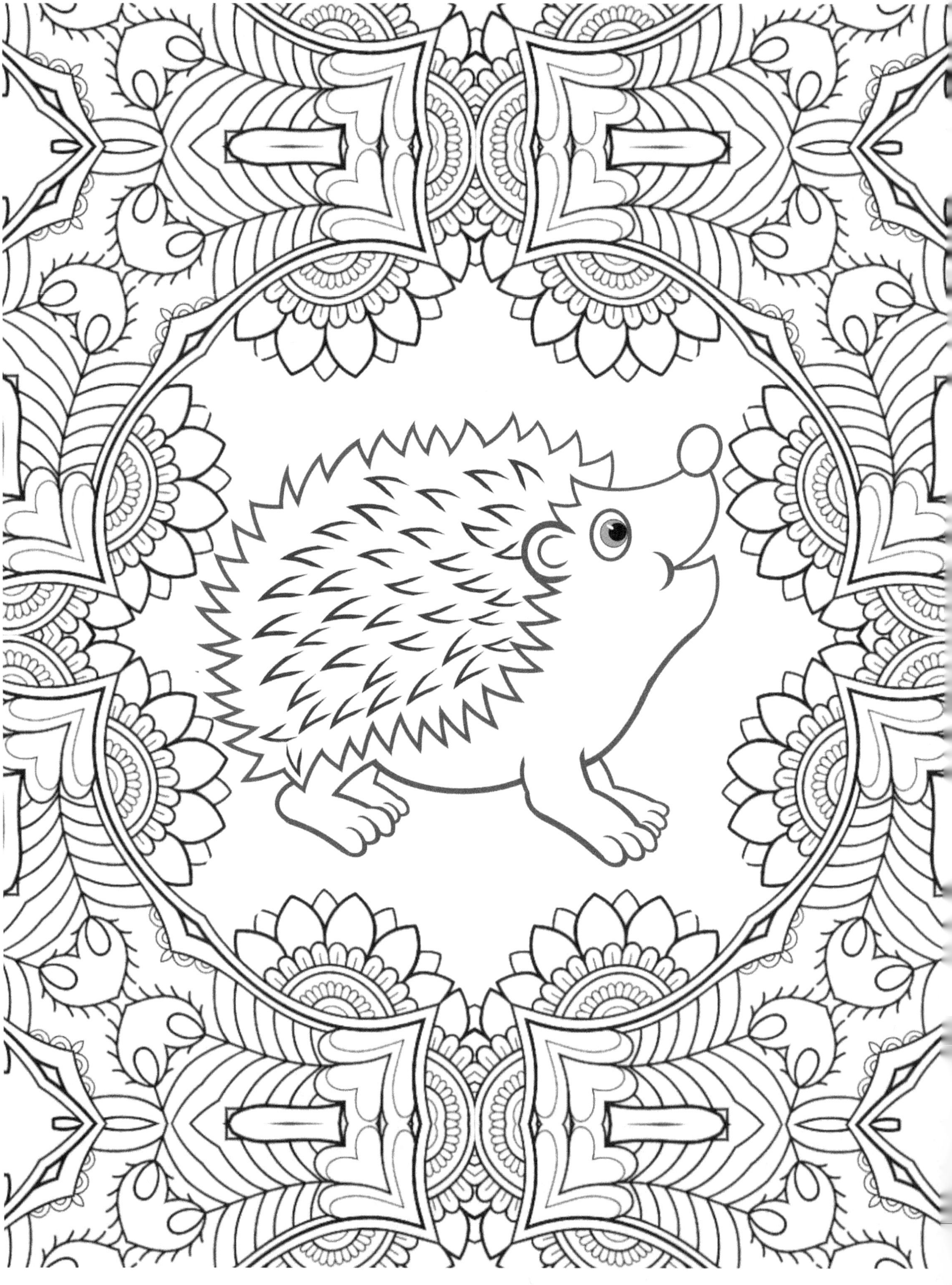

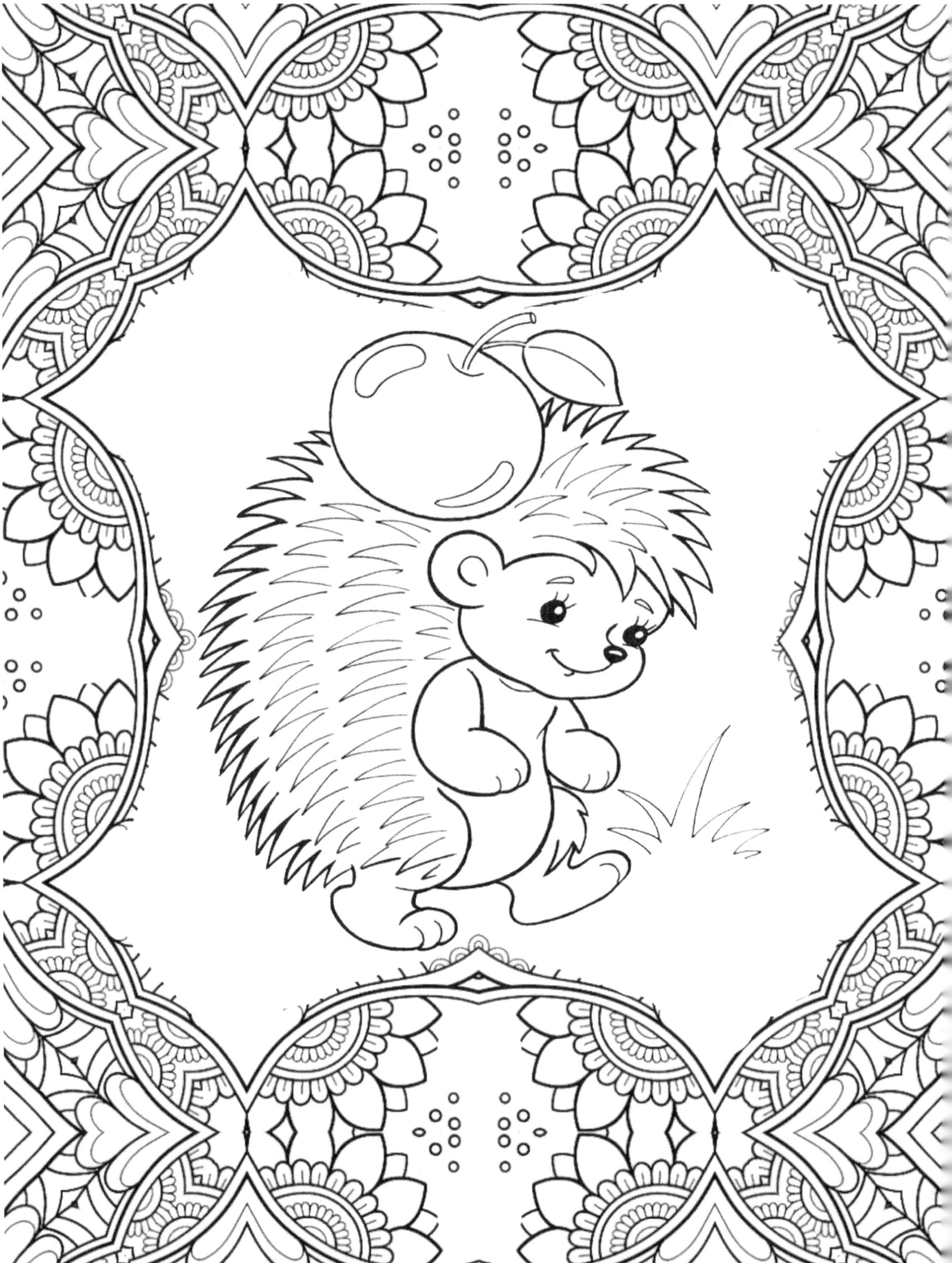

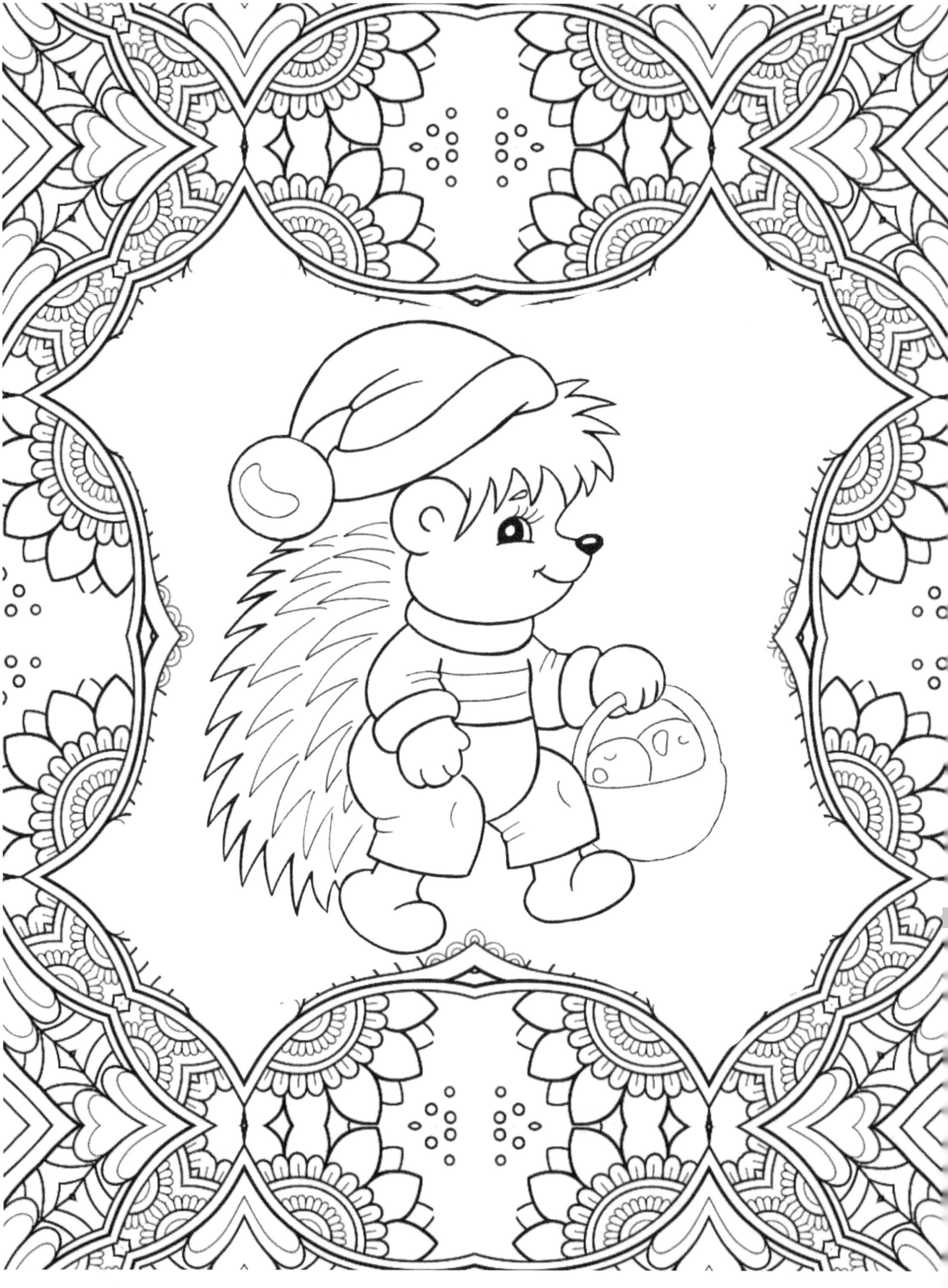

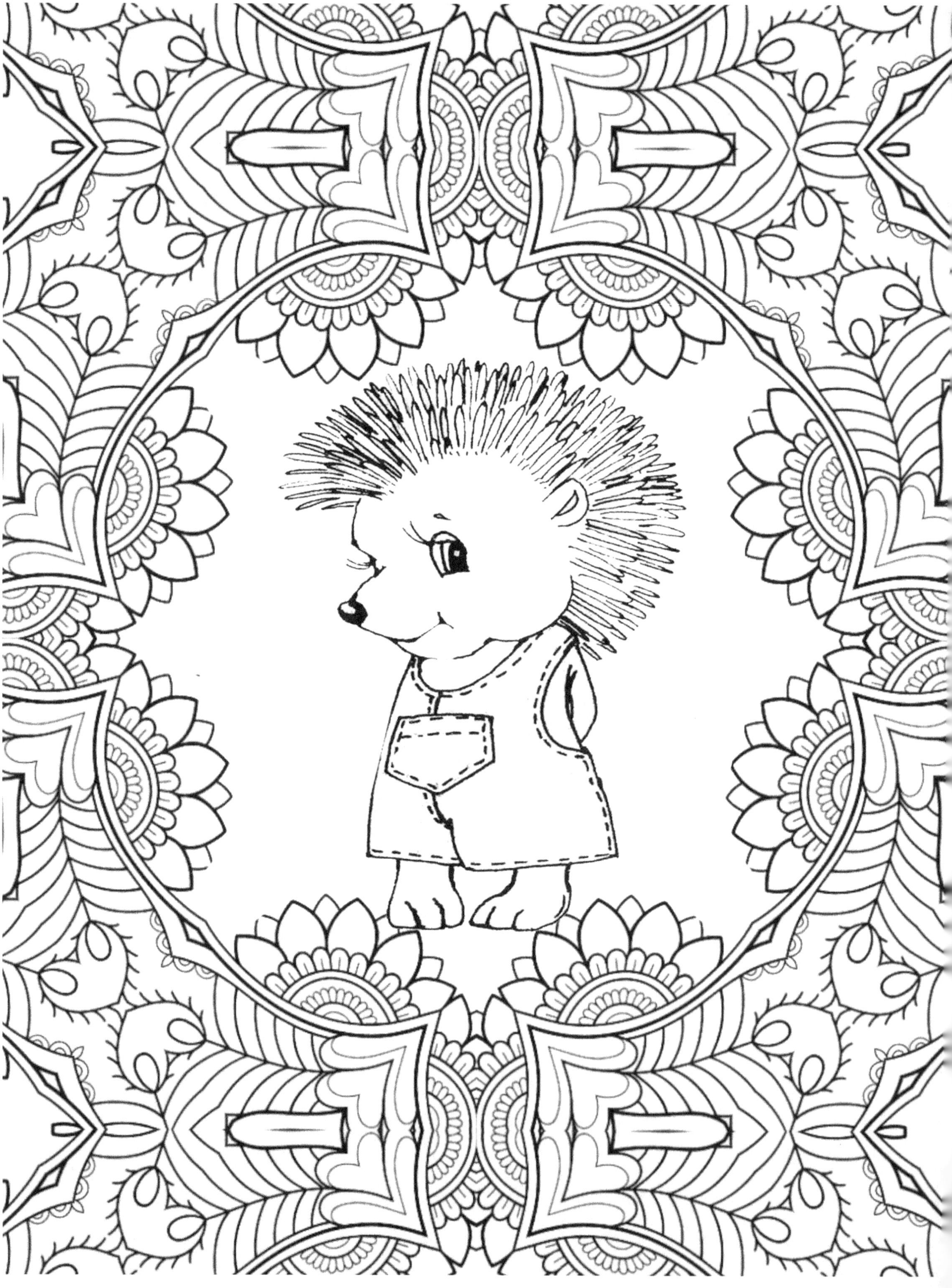

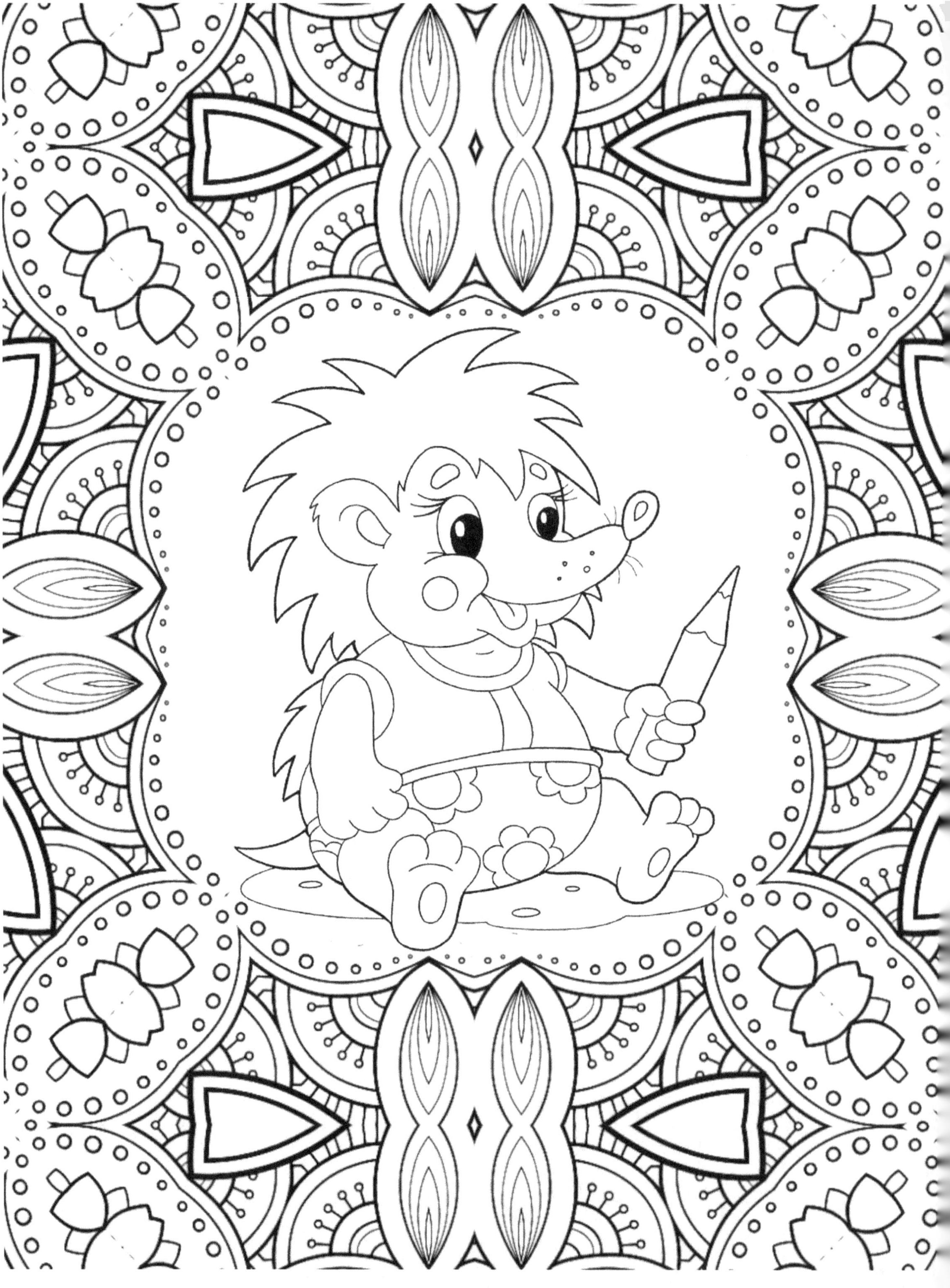

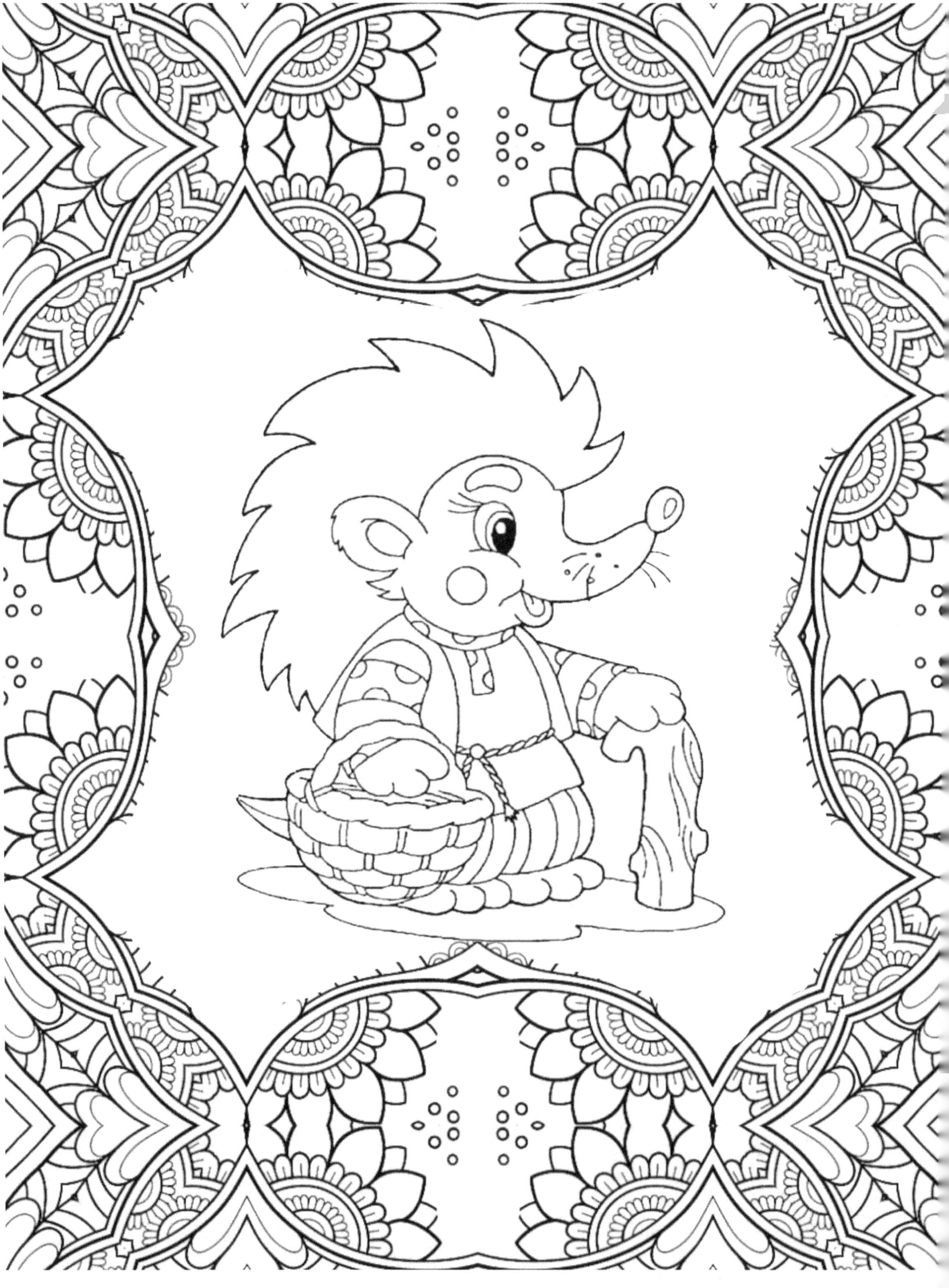

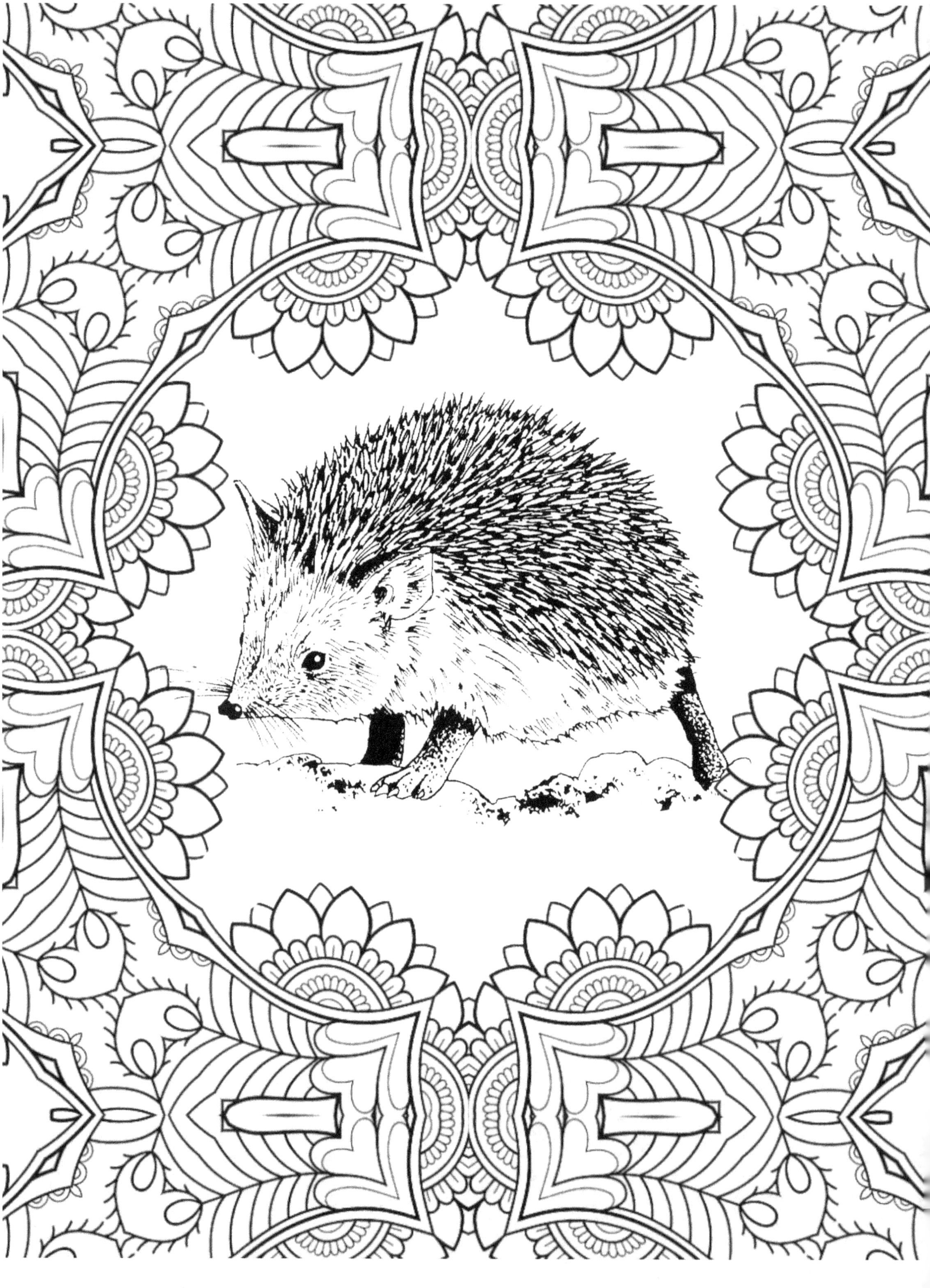

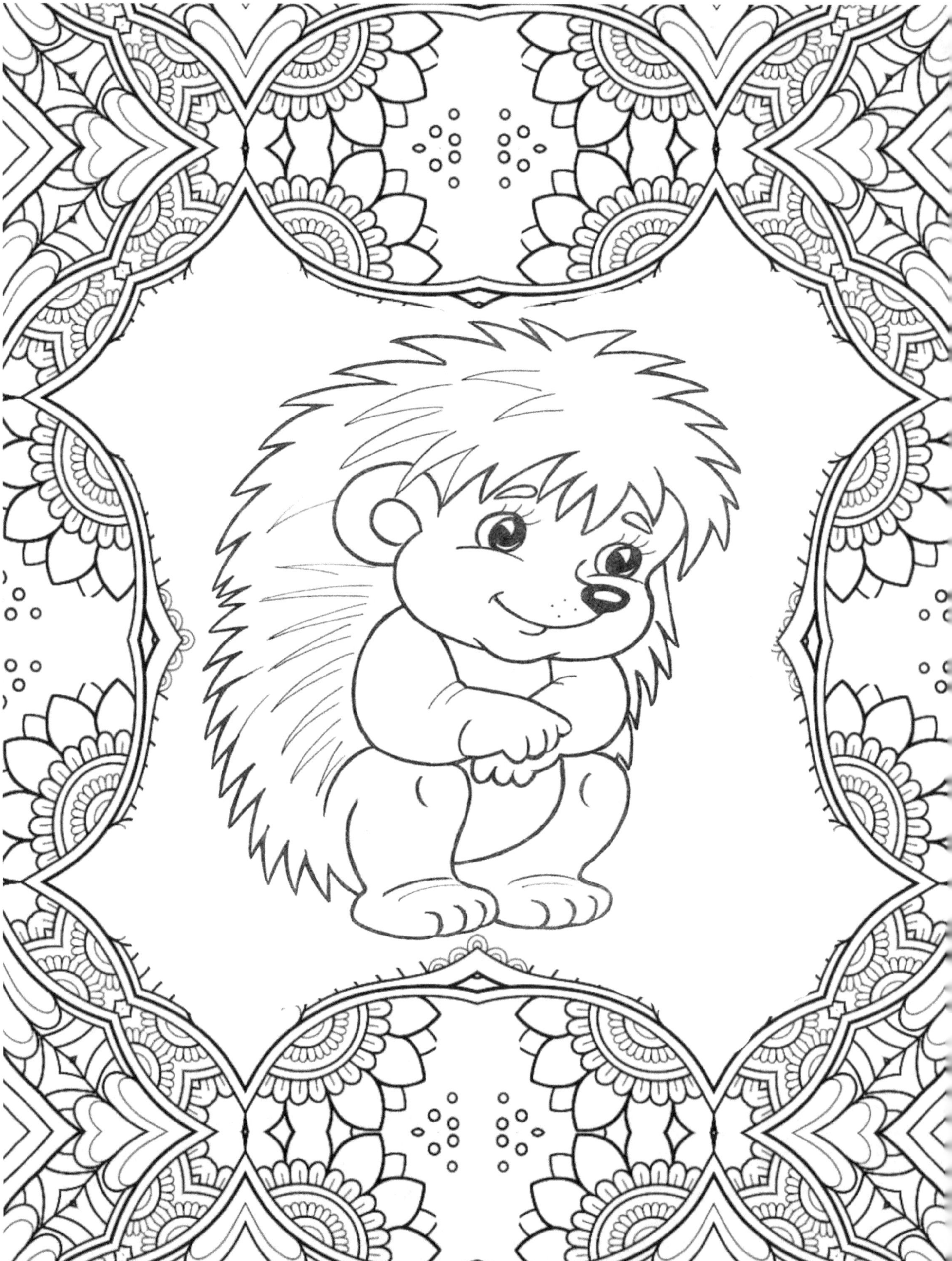

www.ingramcontent.com/pod-product-compliance
Lightning Source LLC
Chambersburg PA
CBHW082153230526
45467CB00044B/3211
* 9 7 9 8 7 0 4 1 3 4 8 4 8 *